THE DOMINICAN REVOLT

THE DOMINICAN REVOLT

A Case Study in American Policy

THEODORE DRAPER

A Commentary Report

To Roberto and Elissa Fernández
For their devotion

Introduction

THIS EFFORT TO RECONSTRUCT THE BACKGROUND
and first phase of the Dominican revolt of 1965
is largely based on articles which I wrote for
Commentary, The New Leader and *The New
Republic* in 1965-66. The bulk of it derives from
my article, "The Dominican Crisis: A Case
Study in American Policy," which appeared in
Commentary of December 1965. For some time,
I contemplated writing a much fuller account
and collected a good deal of material which
came too late to be used in any of these articles.
I have used some of this material to fill out
some gaps in the story. Thus this study brings
together most of what I have written on the
subject, revised and enlarged on the basis of
later information. I have agreed to its publication because there has been a continuing demand for the original article in *Commentary*
and because I hope it may still serve to increase
our understanding of what I consider to be one
of the few inspiring struggles of our time. In
failure, it may yet count for more than some

bitter successes. I have not tried to deal with the U.S. intervention in any detail because I consider that to be another subject. Once the United States intervened in force, the Dominican revolt entered a second phase and I have been concerned with it mainly in terms of U.S. policy rather than Dominican politics. The two phases are, of course, intimately related, but my chief interest has centered on the first one.

THE DOMINICAN REVOLT

1

JUDGING FROM THE EXPERIENCES OF THE LAST three administrations, Latin America might well be designated a disaster area for U.S. policy. During the Eisenhower administration, Fidel Castro came to power. The Bay of Pigs was John F. Kennedy's most humiliating moment. And in April 1965, President Lyndon Johnson had his Dominican crisis.

Of the three, the last was in some ways the worst because it was the most gratuitous, the least predetermined. Castro's struggle for power was a protracted, complex, uncertain process. President Kennedy's adventure was somewhat halfhearted; American troops were at least not engaged; and the President knew how to end the misery, without deception or whimpering, in a way that made him seem to grow in defeat. But the Johnson administration's Dominican policy was, if ever there was one, a self-inflicted wound.

In the end, the Dominican aspect of this crisis may appear to be far less depressing

1

than the American aspect. In fact, the Dominican people will probably look back at the 1965 revolt with pride and even exaltation. They did not have much to be proud or exalted about in over a hundred years. For one of the few times in their entire history, they fought for something worth believing in. Lawyers and workers were stirred by the same common aspirations and ideals. This was so unprecedented that the price paid for it may in the end seem relatively modest.

But the reverse may be true of the United States. Whatever may be thought of U.S. policy, the way it was carried out made the entire operation disproportionately and excessively expensive. The more I have studied and thought about these Dominican events, the more I have come to feel that what was done cannot be separated from how it was done, how it was conceived and executed, how it was justified to the American people and the world at large. For this reason, I will be concerned as much with the *how* as with the *what*—not only with the nature of the policy but the way it was managed and rationalized. If, as I believe, the Dominican events were symptomatic of an American crisis, or more exactly, a crisis in the conduct of foreign affairs in this area, the crisis was primarily one of Presidential power and policy, inasmuch as the President and the men around him are almost wholly responsible for the conduct of our foreign affairs.

2

This does not mean that we know all we need to know to reach anything like a full understanding of the Dominican events. We know far more than our policy-makers seem to have wanted us to know. We owe a great deal of this knowledge to a small group of perceptive and courageous journalists who were faithful to the highest standards of their craft. Two of them. Tad Szulc of the New York *Times* and Dan Kurzman of the Washington *Post*, have written books that are indispensable for anyone who wishes to learn what happened in the Dominican Republic before and after April 24, 1965.* In addition to relating his personal experiences, Szulc was able to make use of confidential messages exchanged between Santo Domingo and Washington during the decisive days. Some official records had previously been made available to Philip Geyelin, the former Washington correspondent of the *Wall Street Journal.* Other references to hitherto still unpublished official documents and testimony were made by Senator J. William Fulbright in his admirable speech of September 15, 1965, based on the hearings before the Foreign Relations Committee of which he is chairman, and by Senator Joseph S. Clark of the same committee two days later. More information from these hearings was revealed by Max

---

* Tad Szulc, *Dominican Diary* (Delacorte Press, 306 pp., $6.00), and Dan Kurzman, *Santo Domingo: Revolt of the Damned* (Putnam's, 310 pp., $5.95).

Frankel in *The New York Times* of November 14, 1965, and by David Kraslow of the *Los Angeles Times* of November 20, 1965. When all this material is put together with all other sources, a fairly clear impression of U.S. policy emerges.

We cannot put off probing into this policy, because elementary political hygiene in a democracy demands it. But there is more to our interest than an obsession with raking up the past, even the recent past. Nothing of importance has yet been settled in the Dominican Republic. The same forces that made the revolt possible have continued to be locked in combat. The breathing spell may be broken at any moment, and the United States will be confronted with essentially the same problems and pressures. More than that: any one of at least a half dozen Latin American countries could produce a similar crisis at any time. If we are satisfied with our Dominican policy, we are likely to do the same thing all over again. And if we are not satisfied, we must know what was wrong with it.

2

MOST OF THOSE WHO ARE NOT SATISFIED BELIEVE that the U.S. Embassy in Santo Domingo was chiefly or wholly to blame. "The principal reason for the failure of American policy in Santo Domingo," said Senator Fulbright, "was faulty advice given to the President by his representatives at the time of acute crisis." Szulc says that the embassy reports "became a key factor in creating a state of mind" in Washington that led to military intervention. Kurzman thinks that Washington acted with the best of intentions but was "stampeded into unfortunate decisions by a panicky, ill-informed embassy."

5

How ill-informed—if that is the right word—the embassy was we may leave for later, but the image of a pure, innocent Washington and an incompetent, frightened embassy seems somewhat fanciful. The embassy was staffed with career officers who had been carrying out Washington's instructions before the April 24 revolt and tried to carry on in the same spirit afterward. A Washington that had pursued a different policy before April 24 would have discouraged the kind of political advice that came from Santo Domingo.

The crisis of U.S. policy in the Dominican Republic was germinated in the first weeks of the Johnson administration. The late President Kennedy had left a Dominican legacy that might have decisively changed the course of what had been, on the whole, unsavory U.S.-Dominican relations. The Kennedy policy, to be sure, had not always favored the progressive and humane leadership of Juan Bosch. It had previously supported Bosch's opponents, who were obviously expected to stay in power. But when Bosch proved in a free and fair election that his people were overwhelmingly behind him, Mr. Kennedy decided to support him loyally, not merely because they had ideals in common but because it was the only way to demonstrate that the United States really intended to back constitutional democracy and social reform in Latin America. Conversely, Kennedy did not conceal his dismay and disgust with Bosch's overthrow in September 1963, and refused to do business with the coup's strong men and front men. Whatever may have been wrong with U.S.-Dominican relations for over a hundred years, the Kennedy policy was sufficiently different to blot out the past temporarily and to lay the basis for a more hopeful future.

Yet, as Kurzman suggests, even Kennedy's policy was double-edged. It supported Bosch, but it sought to take out reinsurance by simultaneously supporting the old military establishment. In effect the State Department gave aid and comfort to Bosch, and the Pentagon took care of the Dominican armed forces. When the latter decided to stage the coup, this double bookkeeping proved to be the undoing both of Bosch's regime and Kennedy's Dominican policy.

Kurzman notes that Bosch's overthrow dejected the embassy's civilian officials and delighted the military attachés. A U.S. military attaché told him that the then Colonel Elías Wessin y Wessin, one of the coup's ringleaders, was properly "upset" because Bosch was "leading the country to Communism," the alibi for the coup. The former head of *Time* magazine's Caribbean Bureau, Sam Halper, who was close to the Dominican situation, has gone even further. The Dominican military decided to oust Bosch, he wrote in the *New Leader* of May 10, 1965, "as soon as they got a wink from the U.S. Pentagon," which, he believes, successfully "undercut the State Department." Other correspondents heard U.S. military officials claim some credit for or express some approval of the coup. The least that can be said is that the Pentagon, on

7

which the Dominican military establishment depended, was curiously incapable of controlling its protégés.

Bosch heard these rumors but, for lack of proof, did not complain. Far more publicity was given to the gesture made by Ambassador John Bartlow Martin offering to call for the U.S. carrier *Boxer* to deter the military conspirators. The net result of the Kennedy policy was undoubtedly encouraging to all those who had symphathized with Bosch's cause.

President Johnson waited less than a month after Kennedy's death to embark on his own Dominican policy. The United States recognized Bosch's successors on December 14, 1963.* This action coincided with the choice of Thomas C. Mann as Assistant Secretary of State for Inter-American Affairs. The President presented Mr. Mann in a way that indicated the new Assistant Secretary was going to have, in his sphere of influence, some unusual assistants: the President and the Secretary of State. "We expect to speak with one voice on all matters affecting the hemisphere," Mr. Johnson said on December 18. "Mr.

---

* According to Senator Wayne L. Morse of Oregon, he and several others had strongly urged the President and Secretary of State not to take this action, and had warned them that "if they followed that course of action they were headed for serious trouble in the Dominican Republic" (*Congressional Record,* Senate, October 15, 1965, p. 26185).

Mann, with the support of the Secretary of State and the President, will be that voice." These words suggest that Mr. Johnson was keenly conscious of his own limitations in Latin American affairs, and had also made a modest appraisal of his Secretary of State's ability to act as his surrogate. Thus came about the extraordinary decision to give the new Assistant Secretary precedence in practice over both of them in this field. To find the Johnson policy, then, we must seek the Mann policy.

For our purposes, Mr. Mann's views on the military overthrow of democratically elected governments hold the greatest interest. The traditional U.S. position went little further than paying lip service to the desirability of constitutional government. On February 5, 1964, for example, Secretary of State Rusk opened the Third Pan American Interparliamentary Conference with a conventional speech extolling "parliamentary government," which he intimately related to the Alliance for Progress. But four months later, on June 7, in a commencement address at the University of Notre Dame, Mr. Mann chose to emphasize an exception to the rule. After paying his respects to the orthodox U.S. policy of discouraging "any who conspire to overthrow constitutionally elected governments" and encouraging "a return to constitutional procedures," he went on to strike a distinctly different and disturbing note. He pointed out that the United States could not "put [itself] in a doctrinaire straightjacket of automatic application of sanctions to every unconstitutional regime in the hemisphere" and engage in "unilateral intervention" to restore constitutional government. Then he gave this curious example of what he had in mind:

> To illustrate, not long ago, a majority of the Guatemalan people voted in free elections for Arbenz, a candidate for president. Later the Guatemalan people discovered that Arbenz was a Marxist-Leninist. Colonel Castillo led a successful revolt and was widely acclaimed by his people as he marched into Guatemala City. Had we been unconditionally committed to the support of all constitutional governments under all circumstances, we would have been obliged to do everything within our power to bring about the overthrow of Castillo and to restore a Marxist-Leninist power against the will of the Guatemalan people.

The Guatemalan coup of June 1954 had been an important step in Mr. Mann's career; he had had a hand in it and, after it was over, had been appointed deputy chief of the U.S. mission in Guatemala City. I do not wish to re-fight the Guatemalan coup in detail here, but some observations must be made about it because of Mr. Mann's strategic reference to it in 1964 and because it has become the *locus classicus* of one extreme of U.S. policy. It provided the successful precedent for the Bay of

Pigs adventure and was undoubtedly in the minds of those U.S. operatives who inspired or approved of Bosch's overthrow.

The beauty and charm of the 1954 Guatemalan operation was that it had been so cheap and easy. An almost ridiculously small group of soldiers of fortune under a then obscure army officer, Colonel Carlos Castillo Armas, aided and abetted by the U.S. Embassy and the C.I.A., had virtually bluffed President Jacobo Arbenz Guzmán out of power. The U.S. involvement was later publicized because the proud and pleased Washington authorities decided to make the late John Emil Peurifoy, then U.S. Ambassador to Guatemala, a hero of the affair. It had turned out so successfully because Arbenz had not controlled the Guatemalan army, and the army had decided not to fight for him. The notion that the Guatemalan people had discovered Arbenz to be a "Marxist-Leninist," that most of them had known what a "Marxist-Leninist" was, and that the will of the people had anything to do with Arbenz's overthrow or possible restoration, recalls the Duke of Wellington's legendary reply to the man who had addressed him as Mr. Smith: "Sir, if you can believe that, you can believe anything."*

11

---

* In an interview on October 14, 1965, former President Dwight D. Eisenhower reminisced about the Guatemalan coup in a way that seemed to reflect adversely on former President Kennedy's handling of

The real question raised by the Guatemalan coup was not whether the United States should have restored Arbenz to power but whether it should have conspired to overthrow him. In order to get rid of a minor nuisance who was consorting with the Communists, the United States sacrificed a major principle for which it might have to

the Bay of Pigs operation. Eisenhower took credit for ordering the replacement of some planes, provided by the C.I.A. and flown by U.S. pilots, which had been lost in action. Since Castillo Armas and his "army" of all of about 150 did not fight and merely waited at the Guatemalan-Honduran frontier for the planes to frighten Arbenz out of office, the replacement of the planes and more strafing of Guatemala City were crucial to the success of the plan. This depressingly hilarious story—an essential detail of which the former President has now helpfully corroborated—has been told in *The Invisible Government* by David Wise and Thomas B. Ross. It would have been more to the point if (a) Castillo Armas's men had actually fought and been defeated in battle as was the Cuban Brigade at the Playa Girón, (b) Eisenhower had been called on to send in an overwhelmingly superior U.S. air and ground force, and (c) if a victorious U.S. invasion would have almost inevitably resulted in a long-term U.S. occupation of the country. The magnitude of President Eisenhower's decision was so derisory that it hardly bears comparison with President Kennedy's. Indeed, one now wonders why President Eisenhower did not carry out the invasion of Cuba, with U.S. troops if necessary, in 1960, instead of preferring to hand on the unpleasant task to his successor. The crucial importance of a handful of planes, operated by the C.I.A., in the Guatemalan coup, suggests how much "the will of the Guatemalan people" was involved in Arbenz's overthrow or restoration.

12

pay dearly in other situations. * In effect, Mr. Mann could get around the contradiction only by pretending that Castillo's coup was somehow equivalent to free elections as registering "the will of the Guatemalan people." Moreover, the Guatemalan operation was the kind of trick that may only work once. It later provided Fidel Castro with his most persuasive argument for totally liquidating the former Cuban army.

In retrospect, there was a serious flaw in the great Guatemalan victory: it had been too cheap and easy. Arbenz was such a pushover that he made thinly camouflaged C.I.A.-managed coups seem to be the answer to "Communist" or "Communist-infiltrated" governments in Latin America. If Arbenz had been able to fight a little harder, it is hardly likely that the C.I.A. would have considered about 1,500 men enough to topple Fidel Castro in 1961.

Mr. Mann was discreetly silent about what had happened in Guatemala after 1954. In-

---

* Mr. Mann and Secretary of State Rusk have evidently never synchronized their views on this point. On the "Meet the Press" program of May 30, 1965, Mr. Rusk was asked about the danger of Communists coming to power through the proposed "broadly based government" in the Dominican Republic. Mr. Rusk replied: "I don't know of any case in history where Communists have come to power through free elections." Yet it was precisely Mr. Mann's point that a "Marxist-Leninist" had come to power in Guatemala through free elections.

stead of holding free elections as he had promised, Colonel Castillo Armas installed himself in power, disenfranchised most of the population, cracked down on all opposition as Communist or Communist-inspired, and invested himself with virtually dictatorial authority. He permitted "the will of the Guatemalan people" to express itself by staging a mock plebiscite on his continuation in the presidency. Castillo Armas was assassinated in 1957, and his former co-conspirator, Miguel Ydígoras Fuentes, was elected President the following year.* Though Ydígoras had been one of Arbenz's foremost enemies and had collaborated with Castillo Armas and the C.I.A. in the 1954 coup, Ydígoras himself was overthrown in 1963 by his Minister of Defense, Colonel Enrique Peralta Azurdia, on the ground that Ydígoras's government was too soft on Communism and Castroism. By 1964, Guatemala was again an old-style military dictatorship, and it had been chosen by the Castroite forces as the ripest fruit that

---

*Ydígoras has related that he was first approached by the C.I.A. to lead the coup against Arbenz, but that he refused to accept the C.I.A.'s conditions. Later, however, Ydígoras and Castillo Armas signed a "gentleman's pact" which included a pledge of free elections. Ydígoras charges that Castillo Armas betrayed the pact and even refused to permit him to return to Guatemala from exile. Ydígoras's story is related in his book, *My War With Communism* (as told to Mario Rosenthal), Prentice-Hall, Inc., 1963, especially pp. 49-55.

might fall into their hands in Latin America. It was in these circumstances that Assistant Secretary Mann chose to celebrate Colonel Castillo Armas's coup, which had set off this chain of events. That Mr. Mann should have given such prominence to the coup in his Notre Dame address suggests that it was still central in his thinking ten years later.

But whatever the merits of Mr. Mann's reflections on the Guatemalan coup, the more pressing question was what bearing they may have had on the existing Dominican situation. Was Juan Bosch to be equated with Jacobo Arbenz and did it therefore follow that the United States was not "obliged to do everything within our power" to bring about Bosch's restoration? Mann himself did not explain what deductions might be drawn from his remarks about an event in 1954 for the problems of 1964, but his actions spoke for him.

The 1964 Mann or Mann-Johnson policy in the Dominican Republic implicitly sought to prevent the restoration of the constitutional Bosch government. After recognizing the post-Bosch regime, the Johnson administration in February 1964 appointed a new ambassador, W. Tapley Bennett, Jr., who proceeded to establish the closest personal and political ties with the new rulers. The United States poured more money into the country after Bosch's overthrow—about $100,000,000 in direct and guaranteed loans—than had ever been made available to any Dominican regime before. And as the original post-Bosch "triumvirate" more and more developed or degenerated into a one-man operation by a former automobile dealer, Donald Reid Cabral, the Johnson administration did more for him than the Kennedy administration had ever done for Bosch.

The other side of the coin was equally striking. From November 22, 1963, when John F. Kennedy was assassinated, to May 15, 1965, three weeks after the revolt broke out, the only U.S. official personnel who talked to Juan Bosch were F.B.I. agents who wanted him to inform them about Communists in the Dominican Republic.* Otherwise, the Mann-Johnson policy refused to recognize his existence.

The United States was also somewhat less than overly hospitable to the distinguished group of Dominican democratic refugees. These included several cabinet members, the President of the Senate, and about two dozen family members and other prominent officials of the Bosch government. Their entry into the

---

* On May 1, 1965, Bosch spoke with Abe Fortas, an unofficial intermediary, and on May 2 and 3 he spoke with John Bartlow Martin, a "private citizen," as Secretary Rusk later described him. Presidential aide McGeorge Bundy visited Bosch on May 15.

United States was made so difficult that they had to turn to the International Rescue Committee, headed by William J. vanden Heuvel and Leo Cherne, for help. The Committee's Annual Report for 1964 states: "None of the refugees who turned to the Committee for help had ever been accused of being pro-Communist. On June 21, 1964, a letter was received from Dr. Bosch in which he stated that 'the immigration authorities have adopted an even more rigid attitude toward the Dominican refugees in Puerto Rico,' and he appealed for the Committee's good offices 'so that our persecuted compatriots may be treated benevolently by the federal officials in Puerto Rico who are handling their cases.'" Apparently the Refugee Committee's representatives were more sensitive than the Washington authorities to the political as well as the humanitarian aspect of the problem, for the report states: "In taking the matter to Washington, the Committee stressed that the possibility that today's exiles would be tomorrow's government justified a procedural flexibility which would take into consideration the sensitivity of notables." Eventually, an agreement was reached to permit the Dominican political refugees to remain in the United States until their visa applications, filed with the U.S. consulate in Toronto, could be processed. A friendlier approach to these Dominican refugees would not have made so much pressure and negotiations necessary.*

In the light of this post-Bosch policy, what was the relevance of Mr. Mann's mid-1964 dictum that the United States should not be expected to bring about the overthrow of military juntas and restore constitutional governments to power? If this had had any meaning in Dominican terms, it would have conjured up visions of U.S. marines and paratroopers jumping off landing craft and helicopters to oust Reid Cabral and replace him with Juan Bosch. It might have been worth knocking down this proposition if anyone had seriously proposed it. Mr. Mann at best gave the right answer to the wrong question. It would have been more profitable if he had tried to tackle two other questions: Should the United States show a special affinity for a regime that owed its existence to a military coup? And should the United States treat with such conspicuous and callous disregard the constitutional victims of the coup?

In effect, Mr. Mann had set up the straw man of a U.S. policy which punished military **18** coups and rewarded constitutional govern-

---

* International Rescue Committee, Inc. Annual Report/ 1964 for the year ended December 31, pp. 2-3. The Board of Directors includes some of the most distinguished and public-spirited men and women in the United States who have for thirty-two years performed an enormous service helping refugees from Communist and fascist countries.

ments in order to justify a real policy, at least as practiced in the Dominican Republic, of rewarding a military coup and punishing a constitutional government. One wonders to what real situation Mr. Mann thought he was addressing himself in his Notre Dame speech.

The only thing that could have made the Mann reasoning relevant to the Dominican Republic was the implicit assumption that the overthrow of Bosch's government was somehow similar to the overthrow of Arbenz's regime. Mr. Mann did not commit himself publicly to the degree of consanguinity between them. But the alleged Communist character of Bosch's regime was the *raison d'être* of the 1964 Dominican regime, the theme which its supporters and apologists repeated endlessly. What Mr. Mann left unsaid, others said for him.

3

Nevertheless, life would be much simpler
for both the United States's friends and foes
if they could count on any U.S. policy to run
its course smoothly. Just as the Kennedy policy of maintaining the Dominican armed
forces *in statu quo* contained a time bomb for
Bosch, so the Johnson policy contained a time
bomb for Reid Cabral. As it became increasingly clear that the money lavished on bol-
stering his regime was being largely wasted,
that the Dominican foreign debt was reaching
alarming proportions, that the balance of
trade was becoming more and more unfavorable, that a contraband operation run mainly
by the military was milking the entire econ-
omy, and that even the Dominican press was
growing restive, U.S. agencies began to press
for "reforms." Some of these struck at the
privileges of the very social and political
groups, particularly the armed forces' top

20

leadership, on which the Reid Cabral regime rested. As soon as Reid Cabral threatened to cut down the over 50 per cent of the national budget allotted to the armed forces and the paramilitary police in 1965, his days were numbered. In January of that year, a U.S. mission headed by General Andrew P. O'Meara, chief of the U.S. Caribbean Command, arrived in Santo Domingo, and soon thereafter, the Dominican command was shaken up. By exhausting his usefulness to the vested interests created by Trujillo—primarily, but not wholly, military—Reid opened up a political void around himself. If the United States had left well enough alone, Reid Cabral might have lasted a bit longer.

The 1965 revolt was basically set in motion by the economic retrogression and political disintegration of the Reid Cabral junta.

For our purposes, the best starting point is January 1965. In that month, the regime of Reid Cabral showed unmistakable symptoms of incurable disease. Economically the country was in such a desperate state that the commerical balance had sunk to its lowest point in 40 years,* and many workers had not been paid for at least two months. † A military crisis caused the resignation of the Secretary of the Armed Forces, General Victór Elby

* "Informan Sobre Situación Balanza Comercial RD," Listín Diario, December 29, 1964.

† El Caribe, February 7, 1965.

Viñas Román, and President Reid Cabral himself had to take over the post. The latter's position had become so weak and unpopular that none of the existing political parties from left to right, wanted to be associated with him, and one after another of the conservative parties hastened to repudiate him. Three center and right-wing parties—Joaquín Balaguer's *Partido Reformista*, Luis Amiama Tió's *Partido Liberal Evolucionista*, and Horacio Ornes's *Vanguardia Revolucionaria Dominicana*—openly questioned Bennett's partisan activity to keep Reid in power.

The outlook seemed so bleak that Ambassador Bennett wrote to Under Secretary of State Thomas C. Mann: "We are almost on the ropes in the Dominican Republic."* One of those who agreed with Mr. Bennett was Juan Bosch, who wrote to his friend, José Figueres, former President of Costa Rica: "We are at the brink of the explosion." On January 25, 1965, another political figure stated: "We have been brought to the edge of disaster."†

These words were not uttered by Juan Bosch, but by an old-time conservative Dominican politician, Dr. Angel Severo Cabral, leader of one faction of the virulently anti-Bosch *Unión Cívica Nacional*. It matters less whether the diagnosis was correct than that Dr. Severo Cabral thought it was politically expedient to make it.

---

* *Newsweek*, May 17, 1965.
† *Listín Diario*, January 26.

Reid Cabral's position had deteriorated so much it was generally believed that he had made up his mind to renege on his promise to hold elections in September 1965. Evidently this belief was well-founded and known to the U.S. authorities. On the basis of testimony before the Senate Foreign Relations Committee, Max Frankel reported in the New York *Times* of November 14, 1965 that

> even before the revolt the United States gave not only extensive economic aid but also political advice to the civilian junta of Donald Reid Cabral even though it knew from its own public-opinion polls that the junta had no popular support and was planning to cancel elections scheduled for September. The United States let the C.I.A. train the police force and warned the [Reid] Cabral junta of Mr. Bosch's "endemic plotting."

In these circumstances, Bosch did enter into a working arrangement with another party. On January 30, 1965, Bosch's *Partido Revolucionario Dominicano* and the *Partido Revolucionario Social Cristiano* (PRSC) signed the "Pact of Río Piedras" in Puerto Rico. The Dominican PRSC was a recognized member of the Latin American Christian Democratic movement, to which the Chilean party of President Eduardo Frei also belongs. The PRD had won the elections of December 1962 with over 60 per cent of the vote, and the PRSC had come in third with about 10 per cent. Unofficially allied to the PRSC was the

23

largest Dominican labor organization, the *Confederación Autónoma de Sindicatos Dominicana,* and a student movement, *Bloque Revolucionario Universitario Cristiano,* the latter the only important rival of the university's pro-Communist student organization. In 1964, a younger leadership, headed by Dr. Antonio Rosario, had gained control of the PRSC, and its policy, hitherto moderate, had become increasingly militant and uncompromising. But, it should be noted, the right wing of the PRSC, headed by Dr. Guido D'Alessandro, also came out in support of the April 24 revolt.[*]

There was nothing secretive about the Pact of Río Piedras. It was signed publicly and published in the Dominican press on February 1. It committed both parties "to act in unity, in a common front to achieve the reestablishment of the constitutional order in the Dominican Republic, and, likewise, with respect to any event which may offer a democratic solution to the evils which the Dominican people suffer."

The PRD-PRSC united front helped to inspire an unprecedented public campaign for the return of Juan Bosch to power. One aspect of this campaign showed how much public opinion had changed since Bosch's overthrow in September 1963. At that time, the general

---

[*] *Listín Diario,* April 26, 1965.

public response to the coup had been sullenly or apathetically passive. This attitude had been most marked in the middle class, among whom Bosch had never had much influence or strength. But the difference between September 1963 and April 1965 was precisely the political transformation that had taken place in the Dominican middle class. One sign of this was an advertisement which appeared in *El Caribe*, one of the two most important newspapers in Santo Domingo, on February 26, 1965. Entitled "Dominican Professionals and Intellectuals to the Country," it began: "As a result of the deplorable political events of September 1963, the country suffered the loss of its democratic institutions, and the trampling of all human rights, corruption and administrative chaos was immediately followed by economic crisis." After drawing up a detailed indictment of the Reid Cabral regime's policy, the statement greeted the PRD-PRSC unity pact as an indication that the people were finding their way. Normally, this might have been dismissed as merely a paid advertisement of the PRD-PRSC mutual admiration society. But this one was different. It was signed by about 2,000 names, most of them prefixed by "Dr." or other professional titles, who had themselves paid for it. That so many should have been willing to lend their names to such a public declaration was virtually unheard-of in a country where one does not identify oneself with a deposed political exile lightly. For days, even more outspoken demands for Bosch's return to power with literally thousands of names attached to them were published, many of them with contributions by signatories of five and ten *centavos*.

Another sign of the times was the extraordinary reception of Bosch's book on his 1963 experience, *The Unfinished Experiment*. The original Spanish edition, published in Mexico, arrived in the Dominican Republic at a peculiarly propitious moment early in January. The first shipment of 50 copies was sold out in half a day. The second shipment of 750 copies lasted eight hours. A lengthy review in one of the major Santo Domingo papers, *Listín Diario*, of January 29, 1965, commented: *"Crisis de la democracia de América en la República Dominicana* [the original Spanish title], a veritable 'best seller' [in English], has broken all records of sale in our country. More copies of the book have been sold in a shorter period of time than any other work of whatever kind by any author, Dominican or foreign." In his book, Bosch dealt at some length with the social and political weaknesses of the Dominican middle class, and evidently hundreds of professionals and intellectuals took to heart his critique of their past shortcomings.

Among those who took it most to heart were younger elements in the Dominican armed forces who were not immune to the social and political ferment in the social strata to which they belonged. More and more came to realize that the coup had brought shame and disaster on the country and that the only way out was a return to Bosch's constitutional regime. In the beginning, and in the end, this aspect of the political change that came over the Dominican Republic between September 1963 and April 1965 was crucial.

4

WE CAN NOW TURN OUR ATTENTION TO THE
charges that Bosch's party and the Communists had worked together for months before
the revolt of April 24, 1965—as allegedly
proven by a Communist manifesto of the *Partido Popular Socialista* the preceding March 16
and an alleged anti-American pro-Communist
radio message by Juan Bosch on the preceding
April 9.

There was a Communist manifesto of March
16, 1965. And a Santo Domingo radio station
did broadcast an interview with Bosch on April
9, 1965. Here the truth ends, and one of the
most cynical deceptions of our time begins.

I have stressed the mood which took hold
of the Dominican Republic early in 1965 because all that followed, including the PSP
(Communist) manifesto of March 16, cannot
be understood without it. Indeed, the manifesto acknowledged this sentiment in its very
first sentence:

"An increasing popular clamor is rising all over the country in favor of the return of Professor Juan Bosch to the legitimate control of the government which the sovereign will of the people accorded him in the elections of December 20, 1962."

The PSP had boycotted those 1962 elections as an "electoral farce." Now, two years later, the Communists recognized that they had cut themselves off from the "will of the masses" by disparaging the importance of Bosch's election and the significance of the democratically enacted Constitution of 1963. So, in a not unfamiliar maneuver, the Communists decided to make a tactical turn in order to attach themselves to the popular pro-Bosch movement. It clearly indicated, however, that the restoration of Bosch's power was merely a slogan intended to serve the PSP's own purposes and propaganda. "As a consequence, the only democratic way that remains open is the establishment of the popular will by means of massive actions led by the working class," the manifesto maintained. "In order to attain this objective, it is necessary to put forward the slogan of the return of President Bosch at the head of the constitutional government of the Republic arising out of the polls of December 20, 1962."

But to make clear that this did not signify any faith in Bosch, the Communist manifesto quickly added: "The return of Professor Bosch to the Presidency of the Republic does not

signify the solution of the national problems."
And, most ironically, the Communists were
afraid that the United States might support
the pro-Bosch movement. Thus, the manifesto
warned: "A similar perspective can induce
U.S. imperialism to encourage the return of
Bosch to power for the purpose of preventing
his return from coming about as a result
of the direct action of the masses, which
would inevitably bring about a true democracy in the country and create better conditions for pushing the struggle towards higher
objectives. The return of Bosch under the aus-
pieces of U.S. imperialism would imply an
agreement not with the Dominican people but
with its fundamental enemy."

On the face of it, this manifesto was far
from being a simple Communist appeal for
Bosch's restoration on terms agreed on by
both sides in advance. In fact, there is documentary evidence that just the opposite was
the case.

I have before me a copy of *El Popular*,
dated April 14, 1965. It was the modest little
organ of the PSP (which changed its name in
August 1965 to "Dominican Communist
Party"). Page 10 of this issue contained a box
entitled: "A More Opportune Clarification." It
was a reply to a previous article, entitled "An
Opportune Clarification," which had appeared
in the organ of the 14th of June Movement,

El 1J4, dated March 31, 1965. The Moscow-oriented PSP complained that the then Havana-oriented 14th of June Movement had made "a capricious interpretation" of the PSP political position as expressed in its manifesto of March 16, 1965, precisely the manifesto that allegedly proved Bosch's collusion with the Communists, *El 1J4's* article had criticized the manifesto on the ground that it "construed the whole struggle in the image of one man and ignored the Constitution of 1963." The 14th of June Movement was willing to pay lip service to the constitution, but it wanted no part of Bosch. The PSP contended, however, that it was merely responding to a change in the situation—the rising popular demand for Bosch's return—which it considered a far more concrete expression of the popular will than the restoration of the 1963 Constitution. The dispute clearly exposed the fact that the PSP was not really interested in Bosch or the Constitution; what motivated it was the direction of the mass movement from which it did not wish to be isolated.

On the same page of *El Popular,* moreover, there was an even more revealing article. It was headed: "Leaders of the PRD-PRSC Reject Unity with the Lefts for Fear of Washington: Reply of the PSP." These four paragraphs tell so clearly what had gone on behind the scenes that I give them in full:

"The Secretariat of the Central Committee of the Popular Socialist Party [Communist] has issued an important document in reply to the refusal of the leaders of the PRD and PRSC to broaden the Pact of Río Piedras.

"In this document the PSP denounced the anti-unitarian attitude of the PRD and Social Christian leaders, and calls upon the rank-and-file members of both parties and the people as a whole to carry out joint activities against the *golpista* [the anti-Bosch coup of September 1963 out of which the Reid Cabral government arose] regime, going over the heads of the political leaders opposed to these activities.

"The document rightly points out that the attitude of the PRD and PRSC leaders, refusing to take part in a broad *anti-golpista* front with the parties of the left and the democratic mass organizations, can have only one reason: their fear of losing the protection of the imperialist government of the United States through obtaining its mediation; fear which is also reflected in the refusal of the PRD and PRSC leaders to push forward the mobilization of the masses, the only road to reestablish the popular will without compromising with the enemies of the people, without compromising with the *golpistas* and the Yankees.

"The people wish unity. And this is shown daily by the many actions against the *golpista* government, which are forging through deeds the democratic front for the return of the Constitutional Government headed by Bosch. Forward with unity and popular mobilization!"

But this is not all. I also have on my desk a copy of the March 14, 1965, issue of *El 1J4*. It contains 12 poorly mimeographed pages. The first article is an editorial entitled "For a Broad and Strong Front." It begins by going back to 1963: "The *Partido Revolucionario Dominicano* [the party of Bosch] was overthrown by the native big shots and the Yankees fundamentally because it had been unwilling to form a broad Front of struggle of all the revolutionary forces." The country again demanded such a Front, the editorial went on, "and the PRD again has the opportunity to head it. But it again fears to ally itself with the left wing. It fears 'what the Yankees will say.' As if the Dominican people should have to beg its enemies for permission to make its revolution."

We need not stop to ask whether *El 1J4* was right in the invidious motives which it ascribed to the PRD. The only question that concerns us here is evidence for or against a 14th of June-PRD alliance. In the same issue of *El 1J4*, there is another article which complains bitterly against a statement in *El Caribe* of March 10, 1965, by the General Secretary of Bosch's party, Antonio Martínez Francisco, in which he personally opposed the admission of the 14th of June Movement to the "Democratic Front for the Restoration of Constitutionalism," because the ideas of the 14th of June Movement were incompatible with those of the PRD and PRSC. The article accused "a certain sector of the PRD leadership of making deals with the Dominican big shots [*tutumpotes*] and the Yankees."

Only now can we piece together this puzzle:

1. On January 30, Bosch's PRD and the PRSC signed a pact to work together towards the restoration of the constitutional regime of 1963.

2. The Communists made overtures to be taken into the PRD-PRSC united front *but were rejected.*

3. Despite this, the PSP (Communist) decided to come out, in its own way, with *slogans* calling for Bosch's return to power in order to avoid isolating itself from what it considered to be the irresistibly growing mass movement behind Bosch.

4. This transparent PSP tactical maneuver brought on a falling-out between the more traditionally minded Communist PSP and the new wave of the 14th of June Movement on the issue of even nominally supporting the "image" of Bosch.

34   In truth, then, the famous PSP manifesto of March 16, 1965, was the result of Bosch's refusal to collaborate with the Communists. And, in any case, he could not have collaborated with all the Communist groups, as charged, because they did not agree on policy among themselves.

We now come to the story of the Bosch's alleged anti-American and pro-Communist broadcast. According to Paul D. Bethel, who has specialized in these political concoctions, Juan Bosch met with two 14th of June leaders, Victoriano Félix and Rafael Taveras, in San Juan, Puerto Rico, in March 1965, only one month before the revolt. Bosch allegedly agreed to "cooperate" with them. This "account" was "confirmed" for Senator Thomas Dodd by the U.S. State Department. Taveras then arranged for an interview with Bosch which was broadcast over *Radio Cristal* on April 9, 1965, on the program, "Here is Santo Domingo," allegedly sponsored by the 14th of June Movement. Bosch's message, it is said, was "anti-American" and "pro-Communist." And "official Washington sources" again "confirmed" all these "facts."

My first act in checking this story was to ask Juan Bosch about it. He wrote me as follows:

> I heard the name Rafael (Fafa) Taveras for the first time on June 14, 1965, when he spoke in the name of the 14th of June party at a meeting held in Santo Domingo. I saw Sr. Taveras for the first time in my life after my return to the Dominican Republic in September 1965. It is difficult for me to believe that Sr. Taveras had been in Puerto Rico in March 1965, and of course it is an absolute lie that I had an interview with him in San Juan or in

any other part of the world before the last days of September of last year when he came to visit me at my house.

But let us assume that we do not wish to take Sr. Bosch's word for it. A broadcast by Juan Bosch can easily be checked in the Dominican newspapers. An "anti-American" and "pro-Communist" message by Bosch would, in Dominican terms, be the news sensation of the year. Until he was utterly dismayed and incensed by the U.S. intervention last April, Bosch had scrupulously refrained from making any anti-U.S. allusion, even in the most trying circumstances, and his enemies for the past quarter of a century would have given a small fortune to be able to use a single pro-Communist statement against him.

So I eagerly consulted the Dominican press of April 10, 1965 to check on this unprecedented anti-American and pro-Communist message by Juan Bosch.

El Caribe of that date ran a minor story headed: "Bosch Does Not Support Participation of PRD in Elections." After the lead paragraph, which reiterated the substance of the head, the story explained: "The former Dominican President was interviewed in Puerto Rico by Victoriano Félix, special representative of the *Agencia Dominicana de Noticias* [Dominican News Agency]. The interview was read on the program 'Here is Santo Domingo,' which *Radio Cristal* broadcast yesterday at 6:15 p.m."

The reason Bosch gave for refusing to take part in elections held by the Reid Cabral regime was that it would legalize an illegal government. The rest of the story merely elaborated on his criticism of the Reid Cabral regime and called on the Dominicans to fight against it "with their own forces" rather than to depend on others.

Had *El Caribe*, which has always been Bosch's journalistic *bête noire*, missed the chance of an editor's lifetime? How could it have failed to report Bosch's alleged anti-American and pro-Communist statements? But there was one more chance. Perhaps *Listín Diario*, a newspaper close to the Catholic hierarchy, had done its journalistic duty on April 10, 1965.

It had. But the story of the same broadcast was discouragingly headed: "Bosch Thinks It Will Be Difficult To Pay Dominican Debt." This referred to the public debt which had increased so astronomically in the recent past that Bosch thought it would take over 20 years to pay it off. The story mentioned that this statement had been made in a broadcast on the news program "Here is Santo Domingo" on *Radio Cristal*, but it did not even bother to mention the name of the interviewer. For 17 paragraphs, there was nothing that remotely resembled an anti-US or pro-

37

Communist sentiment. Then my eye fell on the word "Washington," and I read more carefully:

"Bosch denied that Washington had frequently called him. He said that he had been in that city only in September 1962, in January 1963, and in June of last year."

That was all. The rest of the story was devoted to Bosch's contention that the country "was crushed by a mountain of fear" and his appeal to the people to fight it.

Thus, only three things were wrong with the Bethel-"official Washington sources" version of this interview:

1. It was given to Victoriano Félix, not Rafael Taveras.

2. It was sponsored by the Dominican News Agency, not by the 14th of June Movement.

3. It had no anti-American or pro-Communist message in it.

This story shows that it is dangerous to be too concrete in this kind of game. If Mr. Bethel had not mentioned the date of the broadcast, it might have been far more difficult to track it down.

The evidence that Juan Bosch did not enter into any pact, alliance, deal or working arrangement with the Dominican Communists or Castroites is, so incontrovertible, by any reasonable standards, that one must ask: how could our "intelligence agencies and officials of the State Department have brought themselves to put these stories into circulation or to give them the slightest credence?   .

If we assume that the story of Bosch's connivance with the Communists was a lamentable, but honest, error, it follows that the entire U.S. intelligence and research establishment in Santo Domingo and Washington did not know that *El Popular* and *El 1J4* had been openly and repeatedly denouncing Bosch for *not* making an alliance with the Communists. Is it conceivable that an embassy which was so jumpy about the Communist menace in the Dominican Republic did not scrutinize every line in these publications?

Or consider the problem of that same April 9th broadcast. If Bosch had lent himself to a program sponsored by the 14th of June Movement, and even worse had made "anti-American" and "pro-Communist" statements on it, that would at least be *prima facie* evidence that something questionable had been going on between him and the Communists. But who sponsored this program and what Bosch said on it are questions of fact that can be checked in the Dominican newspapers of the following day.

Official U.S. sources fed these "intelligence" stories to a portion of the U.S. press. But since the writers knew little or nothing of Dominican politics, these tales came out in a form which anyone even casually acquainted with

Dominican exile politics could recognize as ludicrous. For example, one of the chief mouthpieces of these U.S. intelligence sources, Ralph de Toledano, identified "Angel Mielan" as the PRD leader mainly responsible for the Bosch-Communist tie-up.*

Angel Miolán had, indeed, been for many years one of Bosch's chief collaborators. Bosch gave him much of the credit for the PRD victory in December 1962. But, unfortunately for de Toledano and his "intelligence" sources, Bosch and Miolán had broken after the September 1963 coup. Ironically, Miolán had been dissatisfied with Bosch's treatment of the Communist question and had advocated a much "harder" tactical line to help the PRD clear itself of the kind of pro-Communist aspersions that had led to the coup. Ignorant of the true state of affairs between the two men, the anti-Bosch portion of the U.S. press fatuously made Miolán the pro-Communist *éminence grise* behind Bosch. De Toledano, for instance, knew so little about Miolán that he consistently misspelled his name.

A little knowledge of either Bosch or Castroism might have spared these writers from making such obvious *gaffes*. As I have shown at some length in another article, Bosch had been vilified and reviled by the Communists for a quarter of a century. They had boycot-

---

* King Features Syndicate, May 7, 1965.

ted the "electoral farce" of December 1962. Castro's press in Cuba had consistently insulted Bosch during his presidency as a "lackey" and "puppet" of U.S. imperialism. In Cuban terms, Bosch's conception of the needed Dominican revolution derived from the Grau San Martín regime of 1933 rather than the Castro regime after 1959. Though Bosch had lived in Cuba for almost twenty years of his exile, he refused to return there after Castro came to power. After a lifetime of standing for a democratic alternative to Communism, it was not likely that Bosch should repudiate and disgrace everything he had stood for by making a deal with three little Communist groups.*

Even Assistant Secretary of State Mann lent the prestige of his office to a version of a fictitious Bosch-Castroite deal. At the Senate Foreign Relations Committee hearings, he told of U.S. "intelligence information" which had accused Bosch of having "reportedly told" a representative of a pro-Castro group in the spring of 1964 that he needed and wanted its support. This type of "intelligence" mongering appears to have persuaded Washington, according to Mr. Frankel, "that Mr. Bosch and his followers, though not themselves Communists, had entered a 'coalition' with the Castro-

---

* I have dealt with Bosch's view of the Communist problem in "The Roots of the Dominican Crisis," *The New Leader*, May 24, 1965.

ites, who in turn solicited support from two Dominican Marxist parties."* The truth, as we have seen, was that the Castroites had bitterly attacked the Communist PSP for having allegedly gone too far in support of Bosch.

42

* Max Frankel, New York *Times,* November 14, 1965.

5

ACTUALLY, IN ITS INCEPTION, THE 1965 REVOLT owed far more to conspiracy in military than in political quarters.

The first officer to conceive of the revolt was Colonel Rafael Tomás Fernández Domínguez. Only thirty years old at the time of the revolt, he belonged to the younger generation of Dominican military leaders who had been shocked and angered by Bosch's overthrow in 1963. According to Col. Fernández Domínguez's widow, he had learned in the spring of 1963 of a conspiracy to overthrow Bosch and had been offered the leadership of the movement. Instead, he told his wife that he intended to organize a "counter-coup," if Bosch's regime was overthrown. He was soon appointed Director of the Military Academy, but was sent out of the country while the coup was being prepared. After the overthrow of Bosch in September of that year, he was deprived of his post in the Military Academy and packed off to Spain as Military Attaché. Instead of leaving immediately, as ordered, he delayed his departure for eight days, during which time he vainly tried to rally forces against the new regime. He thought of liberating Bosch but counted on so few men at the time that Bosch decided the risks were too great and asked him to postpone taking action.*

From Spain, Colonel Fernández Domínguez began to recruit other officers for the cause of restoring constitutional government in the Dominican Republic. One of those with whom he got in touch was Colonel Miguel Angel Hernando Ramírez, five years his senior, who had returned to Santo Domingo in December 1963 from Panama where he had attended the training school for Latin American officers operated by the United States. The two colonels agreed on a program of restoring the constitutional government headed by Juan Bosch and, in effect, initiated the military conspiracy which led to the revolt. Colonel Hernando Ramírez pays tribute to Colonel **44** Fernández Domínguez as "the soul and spirit of the movement," but the former was responsible for most of the organizing work because he remained in the Dominican Republic in direct touch with the Dominican armed forces.

---

* Letter of Arlette vda. de Fernández Domínguez to Theodore Draper, July 19, 1966.

A revolt was originally planned for the first days of January 1965. It was based on two infantry battalions stationed at the frontier. But when the time came—Colonel Hernando Ramírez recalls the date as January 3—the battalion commanders backed out, and nothing came of the effort. This disappointment, however, caused the chief conspirators to reconceive the strategy of the revolt. Whereas they had formerly tried to start it outside the capital, they now decided it was necessary to set it off in Santo Domingo. As the G-3 of the Army, Colonel Hernando Ramírez was ideally placed to win over other officers to the cause. The final plan called for an infantry battalion to move into Santo Domingo on the night of April 26, 1965, to start the revolt. The conspiracy was strongest in the army, to which both Colonel Fernández Domínguez and Col. Hernando Ramírez belonged, but Air Force and Naval officers were also enrolled in the plot.[*] Among the other leaders were Colonel Francisco A. Caamaño Deñó, Colonel Rafael Montes Arache, Captain Mario Peña Taveras, Colonel Alvárez Holguín, Colonel Giovanni Manuel Gutiérrez, Captain Noboa Gardes, Lt. Col. Nuñoz Noguera, and Captain Héctor Lachapelle Díaz.

Bosch, who was kept fully informed of these developments, decided on a strategy that

---

[*] Letter of Colonel Miguel Angel Hernando Ramírez to Theodore Draper, June 9, 1966.

Castro would never have approved. The Castro doctrine demanded that guerrilla warfare should be waged against the old armed forces as a whole and that they must be totally liquidated and replaced by wholly new armed forces. Instead, the widening split in the Dominican armed forces between the *golpistas* and *constitucionalistas* enabled Bosch to conceive of a plan based, in its first stage, on a portion of the existing armed forces. In addition, the younger leaders of Bosch's party constituted the civilian sector of the "constitutionalist movement." Among them were Dr. José Rafael Molina Ureña, José Francisco Peña Gómez, Rafael Espinal, Rafael Gamundy Cordero, Emmanuel Espinal, Manuel and Ramón Ledesma Pérez, Bolívar Bello Mota, and towards the end, Domingo de la Mota and Carlos Gómez Ruiz. After the "Pact of Rio Piedras" was signed, two of the Social Christian leaders, Dr. Antonio Rosario and Caónabo Javier, were taken into the confidence of the PRD leaders.

According to Sr. Peña Gómez, the PRD's Secretary of Press and Culture, two of the younger participants in the group, Carlos Gómez Ruiz and Domingo de la Mota visited Puerto Rico and brought back instructions from Juan Bosch on the eve of the revolt. Though set for April 26, there was an understanding that any premature arrests or demotions of the pro-Bosch officers would immediately touch off the uprising. This proviso was made necessary by the fact that Reid Cabral's government was known to have obtained some knowledge of the plot.

The authorities knew that some officers at the 16th of August military camp were implicated in it. Under pressure from General Wessin y Wessin and others, Reid Cabral decided to head off the revolt by ordering the arrest of four officers of the 16th of August camp. They were instructed to come to the headquarters of the army's Chief of Staff, General Marcos Rivera Cuesta, at the 27th of February military camp. General Rivera Cuesta had been promoted to the post of Chief of Staff the previous February in the shakeup that had followed the arrival of the O'Meara mission. When the four officers were taken into custody on the morning of April 24, Captain Peña Taveras learned about it and quickly consulted with Colonel Hernando Ramírez. The latter has informed me that the following took place:

> I was G-3 of the Army, and I was in the staff headquarters when the four officers who were in the movement with us were dismissed. Captain Peña Taveras rushed into my office and informed me of the arrest of the officers, and he urged the advisability of taking action. I took stock of the situation and observed the approach of a truck carrying personnel to relieve the guard of the Chief of Staff. I instructed Captain Peña Taveras to forbid the

47

entrance of all officers and enlisted men into the headquarters; I also told him to carry out the relief of the guard and to tell the new detachment to remain quietly at their posts and to do nothing, while we were going to take into custody the various staff officers. I ordered him to send me three sergeants to take them prisoners without delay, while he and other personnel detained other staff officers; he acted according to these instructions.

I personally dispossessed the chief of Staff, General Rivera Cuesta, of his service revolver. The first Juan Pablo Duarte Battalion, which was stationed 28 kms. from the capital, was immediately ordered to go to Santo Domingo. At the same time, Captain Peña Taveras sent word to the radio stations to enable them to inform the citizenry.*

Captain Peña Taveras telephoned Sr. Peña Gómez, of the PRD, and set in motion the civilian side of the conspiracy. About fifteen minutes later, at approximately 1:30 p.m., Sr. Peña Gómez announced the news of the revolt over *Radio Comercial,* which carried a PRD radio program. Another group, it seems, succeeded in making the same announcement **48** over the official *Radio Santo Domingo,* with the result that other members of the conspiracy sprang into action to carry out the plans made for two days later. By the afternoon of April 24, the revolution was on.

---

* Letter of Col. Hernando Ramírez to Theodore Draper, June 9, 1966.

Thus the first and subsequent stages of the revolt were largely determined by the character of the officers who took part in the plot. Some of them, like Colonel Fernández Domínguez and Colonel Caamaño Deñó, were sons of generals who had been military henchmen of the former dictator Trujillo. Szulc notes that Ambassador Bennett, in one of the latter's more memorable moments, had commented that "many of the Dominican problems stemmed from a cleavage between the older and the younger generation with the latter trying to atone for the guilt of their parents who had sold out to Trujillo." If the ambassador and his Washington superiors had only held on to this thought, they might have had a guiding thread to lead them through the maze of Dominican politics. This revolt took place because the Dominican people had never really settled accounts with the Trujillo era, and the personalities were much less important than what they symbolized politically.

In any event, the premature detonation of the revolt was far from fatal. Sr. Peña Gómez reports that Carlos Gómez Ruiz, who was later killed in action, and Captain Lachapelle Díaz organized the first armed group of the revolution. He also claims that all the military posts in the interior of the country, with the exception of that at San Juan de la Maguana, supported the revolt. Nevertheless, the key question was what would happen at the most important military center at San Isidro, originally an air force base about a dozen miles to the west of Santo Domingo, to which the elder Trujillo's son, Ramfis, had added tank and infantry forces to turn it into a fully self-contained citadel of the former regime. At San Isidro, the strong man was General Elías Wessin y Wessin, the main instigator of the 1963 anti-Bosch coup. In addition, an army regiment commanded by General Salvador Montás Guerrero was waiting to make up its mind at San Cristóbal, about a dozen miles to the east of the capital. The air force and navy commanders were also temporarily benumbed, watching for a signal to tell them where, when, and how to jump.

If we may believe General Wessin y Wessin, the condition of the anti-Bosch forces was parlous indeed. He told the U.S. correspondent, Jules Dubois, that he even considered the Army Chief of Staff, General Rivera Cuesta, to be "involved in the conspiracy" because the latter had not taken any precautionary action "and for other reasons." General Wessin also said that he had learned of General Rivera Cuesta's arrest while he was lunching at home on April 24th and immediately returned to his headquarters at San Isidro where he succeeded in rounding up no more than 200 troops. Later that same afternoon, the Air Force Chief of Staff, General Juan de los Santos Céspedes, and other high-ranking officers

50

came to see General Wessin and "told me not to offer any resistance because a military coup d'état had started to install a military junta and call elections in 90 days." General Wessin says that he disagreed and told them that he was going to defend himself against a "Communist coup."

General Wessin summed up the situation on the first day, April 24, as follows: "The chiefs of the army who were not in the conspiracy were on the run. . . . The navy, with the exception of 9 of its more than 30 ships of all types, was almost totally on the other side. Indecision continued at air force headquarters. . . . The police force's chiefs were indecisive and vacillating." General Wessin claims that he was the only one who took some action that night and sent four tanks and fifty infantrymen to the eastern head of the Duarte bridge which led from the capital to the international airport and the San Isidro military base.*

Except for General Wessin, then, the military initiative was wholly with the "rebels" on Saturday, April 24. The difficulty faced by the old guard, which the press soon dubbed "loyalist," was that it did not know whom to be loyal to. Wessin and his breed did not want Reid Cabral to stay in power, and they wanted even less for Bosch to get back in

---

* *Chicago Tribune,* October 4, 1965.

power. In effect, Reid was too good for them, and he was not good enough for the younger Boschists. To the unreconstructed Trujillo holdovers, who had never seen anything wrong with the vicious old dictator until he was safely dead (as one of them, General Miguel Atila Luna, the air force chief who had assisted at Bosch's overthrow in 1963, once put it to Kurzman), the ideal solution was a "military junta," dominated, of course, by themselves, and followed, of course, by "free elections," held under their benevolent auspices. A military conference on Sunday morning broke up into two main groups—those who wanted Bosch back, and those who wanted a military junta. No one, apparently, wanted Reid.

6

If we may trust the statements of the highest U.S. officials, they were fully aware of the revolution's popular and democratic character.

President Johnson: The revolt of Saturday, April 24 "began as a popular democratic revolution, committed to democracy and social justice." From Saturday afternoon onward. U.S. officials in Washington and Santo Domingo urged and worked for a cease-fire. (This was President Johnson's version on May 2. He added one more important piece of information on June 17, which we will discuss later.)

Under Secretary of State Mann: Available information suggested that the uprising "began as a democratic revolution." U.S. intelligence from the very beginning reported that "the revolutionary movement was probably led by elements in the Dominican Revolutionary [pro-Bosch] party" (interview with Max

53

Frankel in the New York *Times,* May 9, 1965).

Ambassador Adlai Stevenson: The PRD, Bosch's party, "planned and during its first hours led the revolutionary movement against the Government of Reid Cabral" (at the UN, May 3, 1965).

These statements would suggest that the highest U.S. officials reacted to the news of the outbreak with the sympathy owing to a virtuous, democratic revolution.

But those who have studied the messages exchanged between Washington and Santo Domingo in this period tell another story. It is not at all what one would expect to hear about a popular, democratic revolution, probably led by Bosch's partisans.

In Santo Domingo, the U.S. Embassy was hardly prepared for a crisis. Ambassador Bennett, en route to Washington, had stopped off in Georgia to visit his sick mother. Of the thirteen members of the Military Assistance Advisory Group, eleven had gone off to Panama for a routine conference. The director of the U.S. Economic Mission to the Dominican Republic was attending another conference in Washington. And in Washington, the Assistant Secretary of State for Inter-American Affairs, Jack Hood Vaughn, was listening in on a conference of Western Hemisphere intellectuals in Cuernavaca, Mexico. The point is certainly not that these men were partic-

54

ularly remiss in their duties; it is simply that they cannot have any particular claim on our confidence so far as their knowledge or judgment of the immediate, local situation goes. Many of their later assessments were obviously based on informers, who, however, seem to have been singularly uninformative in the pre-revolt period.

On Saturday, April 24, the head man in the embassy was Chargé d'Affaires William B. Connett, Jr., who had been in Santo Domingo for only five-and-a-half months. The other key figures on the scene at this time were the C.I.A.'s chief agent, Edwin N. Terrell, the air attaché, Lt. Col. Thomas B. Fishburn, the naval attaché, Lt. Col. Ralph A. Heywood, and the army attaché, Lt. Col. Joseph W Weyrick. The first messages from Connett to Washington on Saturday were not alarming; Connett reported that the unrest did not seem to amount to much. "We thought this would be another revolution," Under Secretary Mann later told Leonard Gross of *Look* (June 15, 1965), "that we'd just wait it out like you do all revolutions."

But by Saturday night, the embassy knew that Reid was in serious trouble. When Reid's ultimatum of surrender was not heeded at 5 P.M., he called on the armed forces to attack —and soon discovered that they had no intention of fighting for him. In desperation, we learn from Senator Fulbright, Reid asked for U.S. intervention on Sunday morning, April 25. The negative response was his *coup de grâce*.

What did Washington want? As we have seen, President Johnson has said that from Saturday afternoon onward, U.S. officals in Washington and Santo Domingo wanted to get a cease-fire. What he left unsaid, and what we now know from Senator Fulbright, is that in the next four days instructions from Washington called on the embassy to work for the formation of a military junta as well as a cease-fire.

There was one more thing of importance that happened on Saturday. As President Johnson revealed on June 17, he and his advisers began to consider the advisability of U.S. intervention on the very first day of the revolt. By intervention, he meant the massive landing of marines and paratroopers that later took place. But if intervention is interpreted more broadly, the United States did not wait that long.

Sunday, April 25, was a day of decision. The fatal U.S. moves were probably made on that day—not, as the official story would like to have it, three days later. When the United States permitted Reid Cabral to resign without a struggle on Sunday morning, it was left in practice with the option of supporting the Wessin-type generals or the Bosch-converted colonels. Since the political vacuum created by Reid's resignation was at least nominally filled on April 25 by the installation as Provisional President of José Rafael Molina Ureña. the President of the Chamber of Deputies during the Bosch regime, and the old-line generals had not yet countered this move with one of their own, the United States was given the opportunity to support the "popular democratic revolution" before the Communist issue was raised. In this confused situation, the induction of Molina Ureña was the nearest thing to a legitimate succession that Dominican institutions made possible. Oddly, U.S. authorities made light of his accession on Sunday but saw fit to attribute overriding importance to his diplomatic asylum two days later.

There is every reason to believe that U.S. backing of Molina Ureña on Sunday would have given the Bosch forces a relatively quick and easy victory. Wessin and the other generals were still holding their fire, many of them undecided whether to join the rebellion or to crush it. The balance of forces seemed so favorable to the pro-Bosch side on Sunday afternoon that a signal from the United States would in all probability have proved determining.

To begin with, there is now overwhelming evidence that the revolt was virtually robbed of almost bloodless success on April 25, the second day. At 10:30 that morning, Provisional President Donald Reid Cabral resigned at the demand of a group of officers headed by Colonel Francisco Caamaño Denó. Up to the time of Reid Cabral's resignation, the death toll, according to the Dominican press, numbered three. Victory seemed so near that, with one exception, the highest military officers, who later turned against the revolt, made friendly overtures to its leaders. The following day, the main headline across the front page of the newspaper closest to the Catholic hierarchy, *Listín Diario,* read: MILITARY DEPOSE TRIUMVIRATE; PRESIDENT OF THE CHAMBER ASSUMES POWER. By military, the story made clear that it meant the coup headed by Colonel Caamaño; Reid Cabral's regime was known as the Triumvirate; and the Chamber was the Chamber of Deputies. An editorial in the same issue praised the new Provisional President, Dr. José Rafael Molina Ureña, as "a man of intelligence, prudence, and good will."

That the pro-Bosch revolt was on the verge of complete victory on Sunday, April 25, has been recognized even by the most rabid anti-Bosch circles. The anti-Bosch organ in Santo Domingo, *La Hoja,* of September 21, 1965, stated editorially:

> The movement which gathered strength on April 25 after having broken out the day before would have obtained a resounding triumph and total success. A profound malaise and an unquestionable unpopularity of the Triumvirate [post-Bosch regime] had produced

even in the most conservative sectors an acceptance of the PRD leadership.

We know, because he has told us, that the only top officer who actively opposed the revolt from the outset was General Elías Wessin y Wessin, the ringleader of the September 1963 anti-Bosch coup. Wessin has further revealed that he had only 200-250 men at his disposal at this time. [†]

General Wessin said that Air Force General de los Santos Céspedes vacillated well into Sunday. Then Wessin told this somewhat incredible story: "I sent two officers with submachine guns to confront him in his office at the San Isidro air base and at gunpoint they convinced him to join us in our resistance." Thereupon, Wessin claimed, General de los Santos Céspedes sent P-51 planes to strafe the National Palace and placed his own troops under the operational command of General Wessin who then proceeded to plan the capture of the Duarte bridge. But Wessin also declared that he saw a message signed by the Navy Chief Commodore Francisco J. Rivera Caminero supporting the Molina Ureña provisional government on Sunday night. [*]

Dr. Molina Ureña was sworn in at 5:45 P.M. on April 25. An hour and a quarter earlier,

[*] *Testimony of Brigadier General Elías Wessin y Wessin:* Hearing before the Senate Internal Security Subcommittee, October 1, 1965, pp. 156-157.

[†] *Chicago Tribune*, October 5, 1965.

though, at 4:30 P.M., Air Force planes attacked the National Palace where the Dominican Congress was meeting. And early the next morning the Air Force attacks began in deadly earnest. And we now know from a semi-official U.S. source that the Dominican military made up their minds to fight at 3 P.M. but first wanted to find out what the attitude of the United States would be.

This was the first turning point in the fortunes of the revolt. From still almost bloodless success—the Dominican press reported only about 10 deaths on April 25—it was plunged into a bloody civil war. Why? Why did the Dominican Air Force decide to attack the National Palace at 4:30 P.M. on April 25? Why did the military officers who saw the handwriting on the wall for most of that day change their minds and oppose the revolt by force?

The missing links are provided in a cable from U.S. Chargé d'Affaires William B. Connett, Jr., acting as head of the Embassy in Santo Domingo while Ambassador W. Tapley Bennett, Jr. was in Georgia visiting his mother. **60** This cable was received in Washington at 5:00 P.M. on April 25, a half hour after the Air Force attack on the National Palace, and the links are to be found in three key sentences.

"All members of the country team feel Bosch's return and resumption of control of the government is against U.S. interests in view of extremists in the coup and Communist advocacy of Bosch return."

Connett continued: "I have reluctantly agreed to the de los Santos-Wessin plan even though it could mean more bloodshed."

And three sentences later, he added: "Our attachés have stressed to the three military leaders, Rivera, de los Santos and Wessin, our strong feeling everything possible should be done to prevent a Communist takeover."

This cable proves that the United States representatives in Santo Domingo effectively intervened against the revolt on its second day.* Chargé d'Affaires Connett was in on the Dominican military decision to drown the revolt in blood and, in effect, the U.S. military attachés urged the Dominican military leaders to get in there and fight. President Johnson ordered in the Marines on the fifth day, April 28, to do the job the Dominican military was

---

* A semi-official report, for which "restricted" sources were made available, has affirmed: "The [U.S.] embassy was asked by all three [Dominican] military services what support they could expect from the United States [before launching their attacks.]" But it is typical of this source that it has concealed the main purport of the embassy's reply. According to this version, the embassy's cable to Washington at 5 p.m. on April 25, 1965, merely "referred to Communist influences in a confused situation, but indicated that in the embassy's view any military support at that time would be against the best interests of the United States" (*Dominican Action—1965*, [Washington, D.C.: The Center for Strategic Studies, Georgetown University, 1966], pp. 20-21).

unable to do. The President did not need about 25,000 troops to evacuate about 5,000 American civilians, who were being successfully evacuated anyway, and he did not need to keep the troops there indefinitely if the evacuation was his only or even his main purpose.

As for the danger of a "Communist takeover" on that day, April 25, the Dominican material is particularly revealing. I mentioned that the two leading Santo Domingo newspapers reported the first four days of the revolt. About a dozen different stories on practically all aspects of the revolt filled three or more full-sized pages daily in both *Listín Diario* and *El Caribe*. Yet there was not a line, not a word, in either paper about Communist influence or activity in the constitutionalist ranks, let alone about the threat of a Communist takeover. The only thing the editors thought worth reporting on an inside page on April 26 was a manifesto of the Castroite 14th of June Movement calling for the restoration of the 1963 Constitution, but significantly omitting a demand for Bosch's return to power. The same story carried the text of a pro-revolt statement by the Dominican Lawyers' Association, hardly a revolutionary body. The Dominican press, moreover, knows its Communists and never hesitates to mention them by name.

Philip Geyelin, then the Washington corre-

62

spondent of the *Wall Street Journal*, who knew of Connett's cable, summed up on June 25, 1965 as follows:

What the record reveals, in fact, is that *from the very outset of the upheaval* there was a concerted U.S. Government effort, if not actually a formal decision, to checkmate the rebel movement by whatever means and whatever cost. Consider these facts:

ITEM: By Sunday, April 25, just one day after the uprising got under way, while Washington remained openly confused and noncommittal, the Santo Domingo embassy had clearly cast its lot with the "loyalist" military cabal and against the rebellion's original aim: The return of Juan Bosch, who had been deposed by the generals in 1963 after winning the first free election in the republic in 40 years. Restoration of the Bosch regime would be "against U.S. interests," the embassy counseled. Blocking Bosch could mean further bloodshed, the embassy conceded. Nonetheless, Washington was advised, the embassy military attachés had given "loyalist" leaders a go-ahead to do "everything possible" to prevent what was described as the danger of a "Communist takeover" (*my italics, T.D.*).

63

Tad Szulc came to similar conclusions:

Meanwhile the events of the last 24 hours seemed to have convinced the United States embassy in Santo Domingo of two things. One was that a return of Dr. Bosch would mean "Communism in the Dominican Republic in six months." The second was that U.S. forces would have to be used in support of General Wessin's troops if the pro-Bosch rebellion was to be defeated.

These two basic judgments, which the embassy arrived at *even before the rebellion could be identified politically, in any way,* went far to shape subsequent United States attitudes and policies. It was Ambassador Bennett who had long felt that the Bosch influence would be pernicious for the Dominican Republic, and in his absence his staff members apparently shared this view (*my italics, T.D.*).

Szulc also provides evidence that the embassy began to raise the Communist issue that Sunday. In the absence of Assistant Secretary Vaughn, Thomas Mann, who had been appointed Under Secretary of Economic Affairs earlier in the year, had taken over the State Department's operations center for the Dominican crisis. Late that Sunday, a cablegram from the State Department to the embassy stated: "We are very concerned with your reports of pro-Communist and anti-United States statements." It seems that Chargé d'Affaires Connett, according to Szulc, was beginning to hint by late Sunday that "the pro-Bosch uprising was a Communist danger."

Senator Fulbright summed up the change in U.S. attitude that took place from Saturday to Sunday and after as "characterized initially by overtimidity and subsequently by overreaction." With far more testimony at his disposal, he, too, was struck by the early appearance and tenuous manifestations of the Communist factor in U.S. calculations:

> The essential point, however, is that the United States, on the basis of ambiguous evidence, assumed *almost from the beginning* that the revolution was Communist dominated, or would certainly become so (*my italics, T.D.*).

But once U.S. officialdom had committed itself on the "essential point," it was not easy to let go.

7

STILL LATER, COMMUNIST DOCUMENTS WERE used to provide doctored evidence that the Communists had been responsible for the April 1965 revolt.

On August 16, 1965, *El Popular*, the organ of the Communist PSP, published a self-criticism of the party's role in the '65 revolt entitled "The Party and the April insurrection." When one recalls the degree of control over that 1965 revolt attributed to the PSP and other Communist groups by the highest U.S. officials, it is hard to read these pages and to believe one's eyes. The self-criticism stated that "our party was not prepared for the armed insurrection and for that reason was not capable of directing it." It reiterated: "In action, our party neglected the preparation of the armed insurrection and the military training of its members." It also confessed that "the April revolution gave evidence of another error by our party." This error was none other than the fact that the party had "assumed a sectarian position with respect to the progressive, decent and liberal sectors of the armed forces." The document claimed some credit for the Communists in the fighting *after* the revolt had broken out, but none at all in its preparation or conception.

The enterprising correspondent of the Chicago *Daily News*, Georgie Anne Geyer, interviewed Cayetano Rodríguez del Prado, leader of the Dominican Popular Movement, the pro-Chinese Communist party. He told her: "We were not in on the plans of Caamaño. In the beginning, we thought that it would be a simple reactionary coup. But when we got the opportunity to get arms (on the second day, when the armories were broken open), we started to fight. The Communists never had enough force to put the revolution in danger. The principal force was always Caamaño. The forces of the Left were minimal—less than 10 per cent. Later we got into contact with Caamaño when we formed our commando (one of the fighting units)."*

Two leaders of the pro-Soviet Dominican **67** Communist party (ex-PSP), J. I. Quello [Cuello] and N. Isa Conde, gave their version of the revolt in a two-part article in the organ of the pro-Soviet Communist parties, *World Marxist Review* (December 1965 and

---

* *Chicago Daily News*, November 9, 1965.

January 1966). In the first installment they wrote: "We failed to see that an armed uprising was inevitable. Consequently, our party found itself unprepared for the uprising and was unable to head it, although as far as possible it took a firm and resolute part in it." Thus they claimed some credit for having joined the fight after it started without them, but they made clear that they played a relatively modest role throughout the April revolt.

Nevertheless, these documents were used to launch a campaign of defamation of the April 1965 revolt. It seems to have been kicked off by Ernest Conine in the Los Angeles *Times* of February 25, 1966. Conine's article was not the worst of the lot. He at least told his readers that the two Communists had not claim :d credit for the initial phase of the revolt, but he pretended that what they had written tallied "on most points" with what the Johnson Administration had said at the time. To bolster this claim, Conine wrote: "Only the landing of American troops, they say, caused the Red power play to fail." This was outright distortion. What the two Communists had said was this: "Only by direct armed intervention was U.S. imperialism able to prevent the Dominican democrats and Constitutionalists from achieving their immediate aims." Indeed, one of the main points in the *World Marxist Review* article was how limited the Communist power had been to make any "power play" or "grab."

But Conine's imaginative little effort was only a foretaste of what was to come. The main dish was served up by William S. White in a nationwide column on March 24, 1966. White took the line that "[Isa] Conde and Quello have now unmistakably and openly identified the Communist party as the ultimately moving force in the Dominican upheaval." As we have seen, Isa Conde and Quello had said nothing of the kind. They had. in fact, said just the opposite, namely that the Communists had not had the foresight or the power to become the "ultimately moving force" at any stage of the revolt.

And now the game of distorting the *World Marxist Review* article really got out of hand. Some of the worst offenders, unfortunately, were members of Congress. William S. White's column was inserted in the *Congressional Record* not once but three times by three different congressmen with their own distortions of his distortions. Representative Armistead I. Selden Jr. (D.-Ala.) prefaced the column by telling the House of Representatives that the two Dominican Communists had stated, "except for U.S. military intervention the island of Santo Domingo would have become another Red base in the Caribbean."

Representative Joe D. Waggonner, Jr. (D.-La.) went Representative Selden one better. He told the House that the "hierarchy of international Communism" had now frankly admitted that "they armed and fomented the revolt last April in the Dominican Republic." The following day, March 25, 1966, Senator Russell B. Long (D.-La.) introduced the same column which showed he said, that "our Communist opponents in the struggle for the Dominican Republic are blatantly proclaiming their responsibility for the uprising.'

Fortunately, there was a bright side to this political outrage. On March 25. 1966, too, Senator Joseph Clark (D.-Pa.) rose to expose this fantastic hoax on the Senate floor. He introduced the full text of the *World Marxist Review* article in the *Congressional Record*, with an accurate commentary of his own.

But this did not stop the propaganda machine. Spanish-language readers were treated to an editorial in the New York weekly, *El Tiempo* of March 27, 1966, by its editor, Stanley Ross, a former journalistic henchman of the late Dominican dictator, Rafael Leonidas Trujillo. Ross told his readers that "we have in the Communists' own words, and right from Moscow, the proof that the revolt which overthrew Donald Reid Cabral was sponsored, financed, armed, and inspired direct from Moscow"—not a word of which was true.*

70

---

* Not long ago, *El Tiempo* published a different version of the revolt. Brazilian Ambassador Ilmar Penna Marinho, a member of the original OAS factfinding committee sent to the Dominican Republic, has frequently been cited to prove that there had been a real Communist threat to justify the U.S. intervention. At that time, he merely said that "the Caamaño movement could be rapidly converted to a

Then a national magazine, *U.S. News & World Report* of April 4, 1966, published excerpts from still the same article with the editorial comment that "the Communists now say" that "only armed intervention by the United States" stopped them from taking over the country. And an official State Department publication, *Foreign Policy Briefs* of April 11, 1966, carried some more carefully selected excerpts to get across the message, as the title put it, of "Communist Involvement in the Dominican Republic Crisis," but carefully omitted all those passages which had confessed how late and limited the Communist involvement had been.

Communist insurrection," not that it had been. But this time Penna Marinho gave an interview to Max Alvarez which appeared in *El Tiempo* of New York, January 27, 1966. First Alvarez asked the Brazilian whether, in his view, Communism could gain strength if Bosch emerged victorious in the forthcoming elections. Penna Marinho replied: "I do not see this possibility. Santo Domingo is not and will not be Communist, and there does not exist any foundation on which it can develop. Communism is a fantasy in this country." But Alvarez was not satisfied and asked another question—whether, in his opinion, Communism had also been a fantasy in the days of the revolt (of April 1965). Penna Marinho thought for a moment and then replied:

"Always . . . Caamaño's revolution was a popular type of movement. That a number of Communists wanted to profit from it, as is their custom, is something natural and logical but it does not mean that there existed a true threat from the extreme left."

71

8

We must now turn our attention to another aspect of U.S. policy which is traditionally shrouded in almost impenetrable mystery and secrecy.

In some countries, especially where the military dominate politics, diplomats may no longer be the most influential or decisive executors of U.S. policy. In almost every embassy, besides the traditional diplomatic staff, we now have a C.I.A. station, military attachés and missions responsible to the Pentagon, economic delegations, and all the rest. When something goes wrong, we hear much about the diplomats but little about the C.I.A. agents or the military attachés. Yet the latter may have a far more interesting and important story to tell. The military masters of some countries in Latin America and elsewhere have learned that what the C.I.A. and Pentagon do may be more important than what the

72

diplomats say. U.S. ambassadors have been known to complain that they did not know what the nominally subordinate C.I.A. agents and military attachés were up to.

In the incalculable mass of words written about the Dominican crisis, very few have been devoted to the military attachés and the C.I.A. agents. Yet their activity in Santo Domingo in the first two days may get us closer to the real U.S. policy than all the diplomatic messages between Washington and Santo Domingo. While the diplomats may have been trying to make up their minds, the military attachés apparently acted.

For this reason, we cannot ignore what, according to Juan Bosch, the attachés did in Santo Domingo. Though he was still in Puerto Rico at the time, Bosch was in constant telephonic communication with his supporters in Santo Domingo. The Boschists in the Dominican Republic were easily able to provide him with inside information because they were strategically placed in top Dominican military echelons and because the attachés' messages were apparently sent through the regular air force and naval communications network, as a result of which many air force and naval personnel listened in on them. In fact, there is said to be in existence a tape recording of conversations between two U.S. attachés and General Juan de los Santos Céspedes, head of the Dominican air force, and General

Wessin y Wessin. By chance, there is also a record of unintentional eavesdropping a few days later. On April 29, U.S. correspondents aboard the *Boxer* accidentally tuned in a transistor radio on shortwave communications between the U.S. Embassy and the San Isidro base, and then heard conversations between Ambassador Bennett and military junta leaders coming through in the clear from the ship's radio. In addition, Szulc reports, U.S. military attachés were stationed at the San Isidro base with the Wessin command and relayed requests for assistance to the embassy as early as Monday, April 26.

Bosch's information was made known in part by Homer Bigart in the New York *Times* of May 7, 1965. On the evening of Saturday, April 24, the first day of the revolt, when the military leaders were still immobilized, Bosch said, the U.S. air attachés had called the San Isidro Air Force Base to talk to General de los Santos Céspedes. The attaché "ordered the Dominican general to have two air squadrons ready to bomb the city early Sunday morning." But de los Santos Céspedes then refused. In a private letter to me, Bosch has added that both the U.S. air and naval attachés began on Saturday evening to "order" the Dominican air force, navy, and General Wessin to attack the Boschist forces, and that another demand for an air attack on the National Palace was made on Sunday afternoon.

74

Bosch also told Bigart that the U.S. air attaché had again called General de los Santos Céspedes on Sunday night and had informed him that the U.S. embassy "had intercepted three telephone calls made by [Provisional] President Jose Rafael Molina Ureña to Fidel Castro asking for military aid." The attaché authorized General de los Santos Céspedes to print handbills to this effect and have planes ready to distribute them from the air throughout the country. In his letter to me, Bosch added that the air attaché assured de los Santos Céspedes the intercepted telephone conversation revealed that Castro had agreed to Molina Ureña's request for aid and the Cubans were going to send some that very night. The leaflet containing this utterly unfounded story, according to Bosch, was dropped by Dominican air force planes the next two days, Monday and Tuesday, April 26 and 27, especially on military posts. One of these planes landed and was interned in Puerto Rico on Tuesday, with the result that the story leaked out again. Still later, Castro was forced to explain why he had *not* been able to intervene in the Dominican struggle.

75

As far as I know, three other sources referred to this activity of the U.S. military attachés. The first reference appeared in the last sentence of the passage already quoted from the article by Philip Geyelin in the *Wall Street Journal* of June 25, 1965. This sentence, dealing explicitly with the events of Sunday, April 25, is important enough to cite again:

> Nonetheless, Washington was advised [by the embassy], the embassy military attachés had given "loyalist" leaders a go-ahead to do "everything possible" to prevent what was described as the danger of a "Communist take-over."

It appears from the context that Geyelin was able to make this assertion, with direct quotations, from the official records made available to him. Whether or not all the details provided by Bosch prove to be accurate, Geyelin's version confirmed the essence of the charge.

The second reference occurs in Szulc's book, where, however, it is limited to the naval attachés:

> Messages between the embassy in Santo Domingo and the State Department in Washington Sunday and Monday had disclosed growing concern over the navy's role and one of the principal functions of the embassy's naval attachés had become to persuade Captain Rivero Caminera [Dominican naval commander] to cast his lot with the loyalist troops or at least remain neutral. To judge from the lobbing of shells into the Presidential Palace area Tuesday morning [April 27], the attachés' effort had proved successful.

It is unclear from this account whether the attachés' persuasion as well as the embassy's concern should be dated Sunday and Monday.

But Szulc also seemed to be basing himself on material in the State Department's files.

And, finally, the most conclusive evidence that the U.S. military attachés were instrumental in getting the Dominican military to oppose the revolt, appeared in Chargé d'Affaires Connett's crucial cable of April 25, 1965 (the source of Geyelin's report above), one sentence of which may be quoted again:

> Our attachés have stressed to the three military leaders, Rivera, de los Santos and Wessin, our strong feeling everything possible should be done to prevent a Communist takeover.

If the intervention of the U.S. military attachés should prove to have been the determining, or even a major, factor in the Dominican air force and navy decision to launch attacks on Sunday and the following days, the verdict of history will be that U.S. pressure contributed to the prevention of an early Boschist victory and helped to plunge the country into a bloody civil war.

The question arises whether the military attachés might have acted on their own or had consulted in advance with their Washington superiors. It is hard to believe that they could have acted on their own because communications between Washington and Santo Domingo were never interrupted. But if they did, they must have done so on the premise that the pre-

April 24 policy required it, that Wessin's tanks and de los Santos's planes had to do the job that Reid Cabral had done previously. Either way, there is reason to stress the continuity of the policy before and after April 24.

President Johnson and other U.S. spokesmen sought to concentrate public attention on the events of April 27 and 28, when U.S. lives were allegedly in immediate danger, the Boschist movement had allegedly collapsed, and the Communists had allegedly taken over, to justify U.S. military intervention. They were notably reticent about the actual policy in the first two to four days, except to imply that they were initially sympathetic to a popular democratic revolution that went out of control. This claim of initial sympathy was never very persuasive because it was not matched by any actions that might have been expected to flow from it. The least that might have been expected was some slight effort to make contact immediately with Juan Bosch, the avowed and acknowledged leader of the "popular democratic revolution," who was, after all, in Río Piedras, a suburb of San Juan, Puerto Rico, a telephone call away. The failure to show the slightest interest in Bosch in the initial period of the revolt was, however, only a negative reason for suspecting that official U.S. sympathy with the Boschist revolution might have been a literary afterthought to make the actual intervention somewhat more palatable. But the more positive reasons for this suspicion are the repeated Washington instructions in favor of a military junta, the increasingly anti-Bosch tenor of the embassy's messages, and above all, the evidence pointing to the military attachés' pressures before April 27 and possibly as eary as April 24 for Dominican air and naval attacks on the pro-Bosch forces. The difference between what President Johnson said about the "popular democratic revolution that was committed to democracy and social justice" and what was done about it was almost incredibly grotesque.

9

When one comes to consider the direct U.S. military intervention on April 28, 1965, one is again struck by two different levels on which the policy operated—the public and the private.

On the public level, President Johnson's statements must be considered the most authoritative. His first statement, on April 28, justified the landing of marines wholly in terms of the protection of American lives. On April 30, he suggested for the first time that there might be something more—"there are signs that people trained outside the Dominican Republic are seeking to gain control." But "signs" of people "seeking" control seemed to refer to a future danger; this cautious allusion to the still-unnamed Communists did not appear to apply to his decision two days earlier to send the marines. Not until May 2 did President Johnson clear up this point in a speech which will long be debated for what it said and left unsaid.

It said, for example, that the United States had worked for a cease-fire, but it did not say that the United States had four times urged a military junta. It said that "we have also maintained communications with President Bosch, who has chosen to remain in Puerto Rico," but it did not say that there were no communications with Bosch until he took the initiative and called one of President Johnson's confidants, Abe Fortas, and it did not say that Bosch had vainly asked for U.S. transportation to the Dominican Republic. It told of the two telegrams from Ambassador Bennett on April 28 that had triggered the actual decision to intervene, but, as we shall see, in a highly garbled and tendentious form. And it gave the now familiar official version of the so-called Communist takeover before the marines moved in.

According to this account, U.S. servicemen had "rescued" the Dominican Republic from an "international conspiracy" on April 28. A "tragic turn" had taken place in the revolution whereby the original leadership had been "superseded" by "other evil forces." The exact transformation was spelled out twice: "And what began as a popular democratic revolution, committed to democracy and social justice, very shortly moved and was taken over and really seized and placed into the hands of a band of Communist conspirators." A few minutes later, the President repeated: "What began as a popular democratic revolution that was committed to democracy and social justice moved into the hands of a band of Communist conspirators."

Whatever truth there may have been in this intelligence, it invites two questions. First, why was President Johnson far more cautious and tentative about the Communist takeover on April 28 and 30 than on May 2? The apparent answer, which we will explore later, is that something happened between those days which had made him more certain and unqualified in his approach to the problem. But the delay also suggests that his conviction on this point came too late to explain an action which had already taken place on April 28. Second, how "tragic" could the revolution's turn have really been to an administration which had never made the slightest effort to support it in the first place? If it was "tragic" that the revolution took a Communist turn, was it not equally "tragic" that the United States did not support—if nothing worse—the revolution before it took that turn?

82   The only other account that we have thus far of the April 28th decision is second hand. It was told to the television commentator and columnist, Eric Sevareid, by the U.S. Ambassador to the United Nations, Adlai Stevenson, two days before the latter's death. In the same conversation, Stevenson confided to Sevareid about a tentative effort by the U.N. General Secretary, U Thant, to arrange for Vietnam negotiations in 1964. The State Department substantially confirmed the Vietnam story, though it denigrated the seriousness of the proposed negotiations. But no effort was made officially to confirm or deny the Stevenson-Sevareid version of the Dominican crisis.

Mr. Stevenson was present in President Johnson's office on April 28 when the President gave the order to send the Marines to Santo Domingo. Others present in the room were Vice President Hubert Humphrey, Secretary of State Dean Rusk and Presidential Assistant McGeorge Bundy. According to Mr. Stevenson, the President read a proposed public statement explaining the move. Mr. Sevareid wrote: "It went further than the simple mission of rescuing foreigners. It included a line that stated the United States would always stand ready to help the Dominican Republic preserve its freedom." Mr. Stevenson evidently interpreted this line as a "hint" that the President was thinking of the danger of a Communist coup. After asking the President to reread the passage, Mr. Stevenson asked: "What does that mean?" No one apparently volunteered an answer, and Mr. Johnson "began to frown and to ponder the point." Mr. Stevenson leaned over to Vice President Humphrey and urged him to "say something"—without success. McGeorge

83

Bundy is quoted as having said to Mr. Stevenson: "I'm in two minds." The President telephoned Under Secretary Mann for his opinion, and Mr. Mann allegedly told him that he could see nothing wrong with the sentence. Nevertheless, the President finally looked at Mr. Stevenson and said: "I think you're right." With this he crossed out the sentence and soon told the American people that he had ordered the Marines to Santo Domingo for the exclusive purpose of protecting American lives. Mr. Stevenson said that this incident led him to believe that the President had in mind "a very limited operation with a very limited aim." When the President committed himself on May 2 to the idea of a Communist takeover in the Dominican Republic as an accomplished fact, the U.S. Ambassador to the U.N. was literally caught by surprise.[*]

What are we to make of this incident? The impression is left from this and other indications that the Dominican intervention of April 28 was very much Mr. Johnson's personal policy. He had paid an inordinate amount of time to the Dominican developments in the preceding four days, and he had given his subordinates the impression that he was determined to demonstrate how he intended to handle such a Latin American crisis. Whatever the role of his advisers may have been,

84

---

[*] *Look*, November 30, 1965, p. 84.

this seems to have been the President's show, and it may have been the reason why he found it so difficult to back away from his original decision and professed motivation. There is reason to believe that Mr. Stevenson and Mr. Bundy were not the only ones in the small group assembled by the President with some qualms, but there is no record of any open dissent from the decision. Some of these qualms increased noticeably in the next few days and may help to explain the sharp zig-zags in U.S. policy.

Nevertheless, the "hint" of a political motive which Ambassador Stevenson detected in the original draft of President Johnson's April 28th statement suggests that the President wanted to bring out the Communist issue by stages. He did just that on April 30 and May 2, but he might have started two days earlier, if Mr. Stevenson's question had not deterred him. One senses in his behavior a straining to act before he could justify his actions. He began to contemplate armed intervention as early as April 24 and even put Army airborne troops at Fort Bragg, North Carolina, on alert that same day*—and four days later found reason to land troops in the Dominican Republic. He almost broached the Communist issue on April 28—and four days later came out with it in a form that almost certainly overshot the mark.

---

* Charles Mohr, *New York Times*, May 1, 1965.

Thus U.S. policy seems to have been haunted by, so to speak, inner voices which sometimes anticipated and sometimes contradicted what was said aloud.

Nevertheless, one thing emerges from the public Johnsonian interpretation: the good Boschist stage was followed by the bad Communist stage. They were so different that the one had to be "taken over and really seized and placed into the hands of" the other, tragically.

Privately, however, officials of the same administration titillated journalists with quite a different story. Here is a sampling of version No. 2 that came out of Washington and Santo Domingo:

> "We can't afford to let Wessin lose," said one U.S. official. "We're not going to allow Bosch to come back and let the country drift into chaos so that the Communists and pro-Castro elements can take over" (*Life*, May 7, 1965).
>
> U.S. intelligence flatly reported that ousted President Bosch had been in contact with several Communist leaders from the Dominican Republic shortly before the rebellion (*Time*, May 14, 1965).
>
> American officials here are convinced beyond any possible doubt that the man who rose to the top of the Dominican rebellion—Col. Francisco Caamaño Deñó—is only a front for the real conspirators, the communists behind his movement (*U.S. News & World Report*, May 17, 1965).

Ambassador Bennett had reports "that Juan Bosch, from his exile in Puerto Rico, was working closely with them [the Communists] in an attempt to regain power" (*The National Observer*, May 17, 1965).

Certainly, the State Department's middle echelon was aware that Bosch's PRD had entered into a working arrangement with the Moscow-Communist Popular Socialist Party (PSP), the Peiping-dominated Dominican Popular Movement (MPD), the Castroite June 14 Party . . . In the days before the revolt, intelligence sources were aware that a Communist junta had been organized to rule the united front (Ralph de Toledano, King Features Syndicate, May 9, 1965).

Dr. Bosch, in violation of Federal law, directs the activities of the Communist Castroite rebellion by long distance phone from American soil (*ibid.*, May 10, 1965).

Captured documents and highly secret reports in the hands of the Central Intelligence Agency show very clearly that the crisis in the Dominican Republic was merely the first on a long Communist timetable for the takeover of Latin America (*ibid.*, May 19, 1965).

Ambassador W. Tapley Bennett told a group of us on April 29 that the PRD and the Communists had been collaborating. He said: "The Communists worked with Bosch's PRD for months. They were prepared well in advance of Reid's overthrow" (Paul D. Bethel, Washington *Daily News*, June 21, 1965).

A U.S. government official in Santo Domingo told a news briefing that "the U.S. government has evidence that Caamaño met Tuesday [May

4] with members of three Communist organizations. These Communists, the official said, 'obtained from Caamaño a solemn promise that if he wins [the Presidency in elections] their Communist parties will have a solid voice in running the government'" (Associated Press, May 5, 1965).

Thus, other official U.S. sources, usually anonymous, were sponsoring a different kind of interpretation of Bosch's relations with the Communists—that they were virtually indistinguishable because they had entered into a pact before the revolt and had sealed it afterward. The U.S. officials and intelligence agencies that fed these stories to the press inferentially cut the ground from under President Johnson's position, which at least recognized a basic difference between the democratic Boschists and the totalitarian Communists, and predicated the Communist takeover on a regrettable Boschist setback.

One hopes to live long enough to read in someone's memoirs the explanation for this strange discrepancy in so notoriously single-minded an administration.

88 Whatever the reason may prove to be, these different versions of the Bosch-Communist relationship before and after the revolt, both emanating from official sources and neither of them necessarily true, raise a particularly disturbing and insistent question: What and whose was U.S. policy in this crisis? Was it solely embodied in a formal speech by the President? Or was it the product of all the words and actions of all the executive departments and agencies concerned with the problem? Insiders often feel that U.S. policy is made like a stew: many people put various things into the pot, and what comes out may not altogether please any of them. The execution of that policy may also be stew-like.

Government officials and the press play a game of politics and propaganda which has become as stylized as an 18th-century dance. First the officials hand out privileged information to favored journalists ("U.S. intelligence flatly reported that . . ."). Then the journalists pass on the same information, with or without attribution, to their readers. Finally, pro-administration Congressmen fill pages of the Congressional Record with the same articles to prove that the officials were right.

The correspondents whom public officials used as transmission belts for these juicy tidbits about Bosch's tie-up with the Communists were, of course, in no position to check their sources. The deals had allegedly taken place weeks or months before, outside the Dominican Republic. But one of the most sensational stories about Colonel Caamaño's dalliance with the Communists was not so far away in place or time. I refer to the tale told by the usual "U.S. official" at a briefing in the embassy on May 5, which I have cited as reported by the Associated Press. Since the Caamaño-Communist meeting had allegedly taken place in Santo Domingo the day before, some correspondents decided to track it down.

This is how Kurzman describes the denouement:

> Meanwhile, Caamaño, [Héctor] Aristy, and Peña Gómez, all of whom were listed as being present at the meeting, flatly denied to me that such a meeting had taken place. "American diplomats must be nuts," Caamaño said, twirling his finger next to his head. "They have Communists on the brain."
>
> About two weeks later, after Washington decided that the Communist threat had greatly diminished, embassy officials said privately that the information about the meeting had apparently proved to be inaccurate.*

The classic case of contaminated news undoubtedly was Ambassador Bennett's briefing on April 29. It was Bennett's first meeting with the newly arrived correspondents, none

---

* In his book, Szulc mentions the embassy briefing on the Caamaño-Communist deal but does not report the follow-up. On the "Open End" television program, however, Szulc told the whole story, including the ending: "Several days later we went back to Ambassador Bennett, I think quite a few of us did, and said, could we have a few more details because we cannot check it out. And we were told at the embassy rather sheepishly, well, it seems that we were misinformed about the alleged meeting between Colonel Caamaño and the five top Communists. This was never mentioned again."

of whom could yet circulate freely in the city. The ambassador devoted most of the meeting to the "Communist takeover" and rebel atrocities. The first list of 53 Dominican Communists was passed out. The ambassador horrified the assembled correspondents with some of the reports that he had received: the rebels were shooting people against walls to the accompaniment of the Castroite cry, *"Paredón!"* (To the wall!); they had severed heads and paraded them on spikes; Colonel Caamaño had machine-gunned Colonel Juan Calderón, the aide-de-camp of Reid Cabral. Szulc tells us that a telegram from Bennett to the State Department that same day reported that Caamaño had "personally killed" Colonel Calderón. The message said that "Caamaño had gone berserk" and had committed numerous atrocities.

This is how Ambassador Bennett's briefing was worked into the story in *Time* magazine of May 7, 1965:

> No one had an accurate count of the casualties as frenzied knots of soldiers and civilians roamed the streets, shooting, looting and herding people to their execution with cries of *"Paredón Paredón!"* (To The Wall! To The Wall!) . . . The rebels executed at least 110 opponents, hacked the head off a police officer and carried it about as a trophy.

Here is the version in the *U.S. News & World Report* of May 10:

Victims were dragged from their homes and shot down while angry mobs shouted, "To the wall!"—the same cry that marked the mass executions in Cuba in the early days of Fidel Castro. The assassinated Dominicans were dumped into crude graves right at the execution spots.

Other reports from the embassy found their way into President Johnson's speeches: there were "1,000 to 1,500 bodies that are dead in the street" and "six or eight of the embassies have been torn up" (May 4); "some 1,500 innocent people were murdered and shot, and their heads cut off," and "six Latin American embassies were violated" (June 17). Ambassador Ellsworth Bunker went the President one better and told the O.A.S. he understood that the El Salvador embassy had been sacked and burned.

Almost none of these atrocity stories turned out to be true. When the correspondents were able to see for themselves and talk to Dominicans in the street, they quickly learned that the mass executions and cries of *"Paredón!"* had never taken place. No one had ever seen heads on spikes. Colonel Calderón was found in a hospital suffering from a slight neck injury and was soon released. Since President Johnson told of 1,000 dead bodies in the street on May 4, the correspondents could go right out to look for them; they found, as Barnard L. Collier later put it, "no more than 6 to 10 bodies in the streets at one time." There had been no looting in the rebel zone.* No embassy was torn up, and the El Salvador embassy had not been sacked or burned.

Ambassador Bennett never expressed regret for his horror stories of April 29. Instead, embassy officers blamed the press for having reported these admittedly unverified "rumors" or "reports received" as if they were "known facts."† Whatever sins the press may have committed, this was surely the grossest injustice to a group of hard-pressed correspondents who had just arrived on the scene, were getting their first briefing from the ambassador, and were still totally dependent on him for their information. They were certainly entitled to assume that no responsible and experienced diplomat in these circumstances would stand before them and feed them not one but a succession of atrocity reports impli-

---

* "The widespread looting that U.S. officials have described in the past simply did not occur there, and a broken display window in the rebel area is a striking exception rather than the routine" (Lee Winfrey, Miami *Herald*, May 11, 1965).

† This belated admission that the ambassador's information was made up of nothing better than unverified "rumors" and "reports," and the criticism of the press for presenting them as "known facts," were made up through Selden Rodman in *The Reporter*, July 15, 1965. Mr. Rodman communicated the embassy's complaint as if it were so self-evident or well-founded that nothing more needed to be said about it.

cating by name the main military leaders of the revolt.* It is also hard to believe that Mr. Bennett was not aware of the dubious journalistic practice of leaving out the source and passing off information as if the correspondent had first-hand knowledge of it himself. As the versions in *Time* and *U.S. News &*

---

* There is reason to believe that Mr. Bennett did not present his atrocity stories as merely unverified "rumors" or "reports received" but that he related them as if he gave them full credence and based his attitude toward Colonel Caamaño on them. Lee Winfrey writes: "My own notes from U.S. Ambassador W. Tapley Bennett's April 30 press conference in Santo Domingo show him telling of 12 people executed by rebel firing squads in one incident 'eye-witnessed by one of our own employees,' of a Dominican woman gang-raped by 12 rebels, of an anti-rebel man beheaded and his head carried around on a pole. Other than Bennett's assertions, no evidence of any of these incidents has ever been found" (Miami *Herald*, July 25, 1965). The contemporaneous report by Barnard L. Collier quoted the ambassador directly: "Mr. Bennett said Col. Francisco Caamaño, the apparent military leader of the rebels, personally was 'going blood berserk. He is busy working off his grudges with a pistol,' the ambassador said. The rebel colonel was responsible for at least 12 shootings yesterday as he lined up opposing troops against a wall in a downtown square and ordered them all machine-gunned. The dead included . . . Col. Juan Calderón . . . 'This is collective madness,' the ambassador said. 'I don't know where we go from here.' " (New York *Herald Tribune*, April 30, 1965). In a later article, Collier cited Bennett's words about Caamaño: "He has gone berserk, blood-crazy" (*ibid.*, May 18, 1965). Szulc and Kurzman tell essentially the same stories, though minor details vary.

World Report show, the worst offenders were precisely the "news" organs that most crudely took their lead from the ambassador; not only did they themselves assume responsibility for some of his stories but they never did inform their readers that the stories had started out as unverified rumors and had ended up as verified myths. There must be thousands of readers who depend on *Time* or *U.S. News & World Report* for their news, and still think that *"Paredón! Paredón!"* was the theme song of the Dominican revolt. After all, President Johnson still brought up the 1,500 people who had been "murdered and shot, and their heads cut off" at a news conference on June 17, over six weeks after he should have known better.

I do not mean to suggest that the correspondents did not find enough death, destruction, and suffering to be appalled. What they found, however, was the result of the civil war, not of a lust for blood peculiar to Colonel Caamaño and his supporters. If there were any true atrocities in the entire struggle, they were committed by the Dominican air force and navy which repeatedly shelled and strafed the open city.

It is difficult, if not impossible, in a country like the United States to separate what anyone, even the President, says U.S. policy is and how that policy is transmitted to and through the press. The way our Dominican policy was transmitted to and through the press in the last week of April 1965 indicates that what this country needs at least as much as anything else is a pure news law.

10

WE MAY GET CLOSER TO A FULLER UNDERSTAND-
ing of the strange contortions of U.S. policy
in the Dominican crisis by observing a peculiar phenomenon—the almost obsessive in-
sistence on the part of the highest U.S. officials
that they did not do what they did and that
they did what they did not do.

"Let me also make clear tonight that we
support no single man or any single group of
men in the Dominican Republic." said President Johnson on May 2. The United States,
Thomas Mann told Max Frankel in the New
York *Times* of May 9, did not respond to a request from the military junta formed April 28
to send in U.S. armed forces "because this
would have amounted to taking sides in the
internal struggle." Five months later, on October 12 in San Diego, Mr. Mann again insisted
that "in the case of the Dominican Republic
we refrained, during the first days of violence,

from 'supporting' the outgoing government or 'supporting' either of the factions contending for power." Throughout, "neutrality," "non-intervention," self-imposed abstention from "supporting" anyone or any cause was an article of faith.

One asks not merely whether this was true, but whether it was fitting. Whatever a great power like the United States did or did not do in the Dominican Republic, it could not help influencing the course of events. Ever since Secretary of State William H. Seward tried to annex the Dominican Republic to the United States a hundred years ago, the United States has partly or wholly determined the Dominicans' fate. A U.S. "receivership" of Dominican finances was imposed in 1905; a U.S. military occupation lasted from 1916 to 1924; Trujillo's tyranny was favored for almost two decades; when the old despot decided to bite the hand that had fed him, the C.I.A. provided the weapons for his assassination; and U.S. official representatives have taken a hand in every succeeding change of government. After all this, it was really too much to promise and pretend and protest that we supported no one in the very act of supporting the wrong ones.

We may hold in abeyance the question of whether the military attachés incited the Dominican armed forces to fight the Boschist revolt in the first days. But there can be no doubt that Ambassador Bennett himself soon arranged for matériel support in behalf of the military junta.

The story can be pieced together from several sources. On Monday, April 26, according to Szulc, U.S. military attachés at the San Isidro base, General Wessin's command post, relayed to the embassy requests for communications equipment, particularly for walkie-talkies, to coordinate the action of Wessin's tanks. Szulc then refers to a long cablegram from Chargé d'Affaires Connett to the State Department that afternoon, and paraphrases its contents as follows:

> that while direct United States intervention in the Dominican civil war might be inadvisable because of Dr. Bosch's popularity, the pro-Bosch movement had to be stopped by other means—or there would be "extremism in six months" in the Dominican Republic. The cablegram implied in effect that at least logistical support should be given the Wessin forces.

And logistical support was given the Wessin forces. Ambassador Bennett returned to Santo Domingo at about noon on Tuesday, April 27. Szulc goes on:

> One of the ambassador's first acts after he got behind his desk was to send a cablegram to Washington recommending that walkie-talkies and other communications equipment be flown in for the Wessin forces. He indicated that the availability of such equipment could spell the difference between victory or defeat for Wessin.

Philip Geyelin of the *Wall Street Journal* (June 25, 1965) had previously derived similar information from the official records:

> While Washington continued to proclaim impartiality and to decry continued bloodshed, the Santo Domingo embassy, by Wednesday [April 28], was even more actively laboring in the "loyalist" cause. Communications gear was urgently requested, to help the isolated anti-rebel units maintain closer contact.
>
> Though regretting the necessity for a "military solution for a political crisis," the embassy went on to warn, in the afternoon of the day marines finally landed [April 28], that denial of communications help could so dishearten the junta forces that U.S. military intervention might well be recommended "in the near future" to protect citizens and possibly for other purposes. Pointedly, Washington was asked to make a choice.

Geyelin, it is clear, had known whereof he had written. Szulc's book gives the exact time and language of Ambassador Bennett's message. As the newly formed three-man military junta headed by Colonel Pédro Bartolome Benoit of the Dominican air force began to see victory slip from its grasp on the morning of April 28, its desperation became infectious. At 1:48 P.M., Ambassador Bennett cabled the State Department that Wessin's communications problem was "critical." He reminded the department that "these people are facing leftist forces" and asked the department to real-

100

ize "what would be the effect on the morale of the air force and others" if their requests were rejected.

Shortly afterward, Ambassador Bennett sent this message to Washington:

I regret that we may have to impose a military solution to a political problem . . . While leftist propaganda will fuzz this up as a fight between the military and the people, the issue is really between those who want a Castro-type solution and those who oppose it.

I don't want to overdramatize, but if we deny the communications equipment, and if the opposition to the leftists lose heart, we may be asking in the near future for a landing of marines to protect U.S. interests and for other purposes. What does Washington prefer?

It should be remembered that the ambassador had barely been back in Santo Domingo for twenty-four hours. His concern was entirely political, not "humanitarian." His language was so vague that it seemed designed to take in far more than genuine Communists. "Those who want a Castro-type solution" was a peculiar circumlocution if he meant bona-fide Castroites, and "leftists" might easily have embraced anyone to the left of Reid Cabral or General Wessin. We have here a diplomat who was not necessarily unbalanced by panic or misinformation but rather had been conditioned to take a certain course of action by his general background and previous U.S. policy.

101

So far in this incident I have cited correspondents who had some access to official records. The rest of the story can be told in the words of two leading members of the Senate Foreign Relations Committee who undoubtedly knew what was in the diplomatic files. On September 15, 1965, Senator Fulbright declared:

> Ambassador Bennett thereupon [the morning of April 28] urgently recommended that the anti-rebels under Air Force General de los Santos be furnished 50 walkie-talkies from U.S. Defense Department stocks in Puerto Rico. Repeating this recommendation later in the day, Bennett said that the issue was one between Castroism and its opponents.

Another member of the Foreign Relations Committee, Senator Joseph Clark of Pennsylvania, assured the Senate two days later: "I can testify from my own personal knowledge that the comments of the Senator from Arkansas [Fulbright] are fully and accurately documented by the classified record in the files of the Committee on Foreign Relations." On the incident in question, Senator Clark went on to say: "Ambassador Bennett requested walkie-talkies for the military junta, and he got them."

As for the origin of the three-man junta, Senator Clark also lifted the veil a little higher:

> At the instance of the C.I.A.—I believe it can

be documented—a new junta headed by a certain Colonel Benoit had been formed, although it was pretty well confined to the San Isidro air base.

Thus Ambassador Bennett was under pressure from two directions—from the military attachés stationed with Wessin's forces and from a Dominican military junta behind which was the C.I.A.

One thing, however, may be said in behalf of this episode of the walkie-talkies—it was never mentioned by President Johnson, Secretary Rusk, Under Secretary Mann, or anyone else in an official position, and so they cannot be accused of having misrepresented it. Unfortunately, the President could not similarly ignore the actual request from Colonel Benoit for U.S. military intervention or tell the whole story. As I have previously mentioned, it appears that he told it in a garbled and tendentious form.

As Mr. Johnson reminisced on May 2 and May 4, he was sitting in his office on the afternoon of Wednesday, April 28, with Secretary of State Rusk, Secretary of Defense McNamara, and Presidential Assistant McGeorge Bundy, and with "no desire to interfere" in the Dominican Republic. Suddenly, shortly after 3 P.M. he received a cable from Ambassador Bennett that the police chief of Santo Domingo and "govermental authorities" had informed him that they "could no longer protect us" (May 2). The same cable also stated that the ambassador was "not prepared at this moment to recommend that you take this action" and merely wished to alert Washington to the necessity of contingency planning (May 4). About two hours later, at 5:14 P.M., another cable from Ambassador Bennett repeated that the Dominican "police and the government" could no longer guarantee American or foreign lives, but this time the ambassador went on to say that "only an immediate landing of American forces could safeguard and protect" them (May 2); or in the later version, a cable at 5:16 P.M. said "there is firing in the streets, there is great danger to all personnel in this area, land the troops immediately to protect our people" (May 4). The same two cables were described in more or less the same way by Secretary Rusk on May 26.

I would recommend the sequence of events on April 28 to a graduate seminar in history as a classical case study of three stages of historical events: what actually happened, what is at first said to have happened, and what later comes out as having really happened.

Our seminar might well start with the events of the previous day, Tuesday, April 27. That morning an incident took place at the Hotel Embajador which later became, in a distorted form, the main exhibit to support the contention that a landing of marines had been necessary to save American lives. Over 1,000 Americans were assembled at the hotel waiting for evacuation. A group of armed "rebels" burst into the lobby obviously looking for someone, lined up the naturally frightened American civilians against the walls, and fired some shots in the air. When they did not find what they were looking for the intruders left, the evacuation of 1,172 Americans went off on schedule, and except for some frayed nerves, no one was any the worse for the experience.

The class will please note how easy it is, in the heat of defending a policy, to get even the date of a key event wrong. On May 26, a month later, Secretary of State Rusk referred to the Hotel Embajador incident in order to impress his audience with the grave peril to "hundreds" of Americans at the moment the President received the second telegram from Ambassador Bennett at 5:15 P.M. on Wednesday, April 28.* The Secretary said: "That is, that telegram indicated that there was a most immediate problem on the scene. Hundreds

---

* This is, of course, the same telegram that the President said was received at 5:14 P.M. on May 2 and 5:16 P.M. on May 4. Since the *Department of State Bulletin* of May 17, May 24 and June 14, 1965, contains the official texts with the three slightly different times of arrival, I have thought it best to cite them in the same way.

were gathered at the Embajador Hotel, and there were people running around the hotel, shooting it up with tommyguns, and so forth." This incident had actually happened over twenty-four hours before the telegram was received, but it apparently meant so much to the Secretary that he unwittingly juxtaposed it with the famous "critic" telegram.

If the incident signified anything, however, it was that the rebels had not been bent on harming Americans. With over a thousand Americans at their mercy in the hotel, they could easily have done more than at worst to have given them a good scare. It later transpired that the rebel band had been looking for Rafael Bonilla Aybar, publisher of the newspaper, *Prensa Libre,* as close to a fascist sheet as has existed in Latin America. In short, the incident was not anti-American in origin; it was a typical, short-lived contretemps in the midst of a civil war; and it had a happy ending.

It is noteworthy that Ambassador Bennett's cable to Washington three or four hours later that same day intimating that the marines might have to be called soon, did not owe its inspiration to the Hotel Embajador incident, as one might have expected if saving U.S. lives had been uppermost in his mind. His entire argument, as we have seen, took off from the urgent need of the Wessin forces for "communications equipment," the denial of which might so make them "lose heart" that the marines instead of the Dominican armed forces might have to "protect U.S. interests and *for other purposes*" (my italics, T.D.). Indeed, from the moment he stepped back into the embassy at about noon on April 27, Ambassador Bennett followed a coldly consistent, ruthlessly rational line. From the first, the ambassador told Washington what it had to do to make possible a military junta victory or, failing that, to frustrate a revolutionary victory. It was not his fault that, for political reasons, Washington decided to "fuzz" the real issue as he saw it and which he stated with tough-minded clarity in his cable of April 27, before there was any reason for him to become panic-stricken.

In fact, soon after Mr. Bennett had sent the plea for walkie-talkies on April 27, he had every reason to believe that Wessin's forces had turned the tables on the revolutionaries and had victory in their grasp. One of the initial advantages of the revolt had been the hesitations and dissensions within the armed forces' command.* By April 27, however, the vacillators had made up their minds. The Dominican navy as a whole cast in with the

---

* In an interview with Jules Dubois of the Chicago *Tribune* (April 30, 1965), General Wessin complained rancorously about the other Dominican commanders. He had "bitter words about" General Marco Rivera Cuesta, whom he accused of having been "lax about the conspiracy." When asked by Dubois why

old regime. General Montás Guerrero decided to jump off the fence and sent his regiment from San Cristóbal into the western sector of the capital, not far from the Hotel Embajador. Wessin's tanks staged a major push to get into the city from the east across the Duarte bridge. In any event, the outlook seemed so unfavorable to the rebel leaders by the late afternoon that a group of them, including Provisional President Molina Ureña and Colonel Caamaño, came to the U.S. Embassy to ask the ambassador to mediate and negotiate a settlement.

This meeting has given rise to such conflicting accounts that there is no way to recapture it to the satisfaction of both sides. In brief, Mr. Bennett says that he refused the request for mediation and negotiation because they would have amounted to "intervention," for which he lacked authorization. Colonel Caamaño claims that Mr. Bennett told them not to try to negotiate but to surrender outright. The only thing both seem to agree on is that the ambassador refused the request to me-

---

he had not attacked on Sunday morning as ordered to do by Reid Cabral, Wessin replied: "The navy started in this with us and then decided to be neutral. The same happened with the air force. Then a group of officers of the air force were ready to surrender and accept the conditions of the rebels." General Wessin asserted that "had he failed to convince the reluctant air force and army chiefs to attack the Communists at 6 A.M. Monday, the Reds would have been in power that night." These complaints suggest that a great deal of pressure must have been necessary to get the air force, navy, and army chiefs to fight.

diate and negotiate, which is enough for our purposes. Sr. Molina Ureña decided to take asylum in a Latin American embassy. Overcome by fatigue, Colonel Hernando Ramírez also went into asylum and handed the top rebel command to Colonel Caamaño.

There was nothing panicky or ill informed about Mr. Bennett's refusal to mediate. With virtually the whole rebel command in his office asking, in effect, for a face-saving end to the revolt, he had every right to consider it all but over. The only question was whether he would make it easier for them. The reason he has given for telling them to do it the hard way is so unconvincing that one is forced to seek another explanation. He was so little loath to "intervene" that he had spent a good part of that afternoon trying to persuade Washington to save Wessin's forces from possible defeat by giving them what seemed to be desperately needed communications equipment. Instead of similarly seeking authorization from Washington to accede to the request for mediation, he merely rejected it on the ground that he lacked authorization. Given the documentary evidence of the lengths to which the ambassador was willing to go to bring about a rebel defeat, it is hard to believe that fastidiousness in his interpretation of intervention was his real motive. More probably, he did not wish to drag out the apparent rebel defeat by interposing a period of negotiation, and preferred to leave the rebel leaders to the tender mercies of the old *trujillista* generals without accepting any responsibility for them.

This was the second time in three days that a U.S. action may have served to prolong the conflict. On April 24 and 25, the U.S. military attachés may have kept the war going by egging on the Dominican military leaders. On April 27, Ambassador Bennett almost certainly kept the war going by refusing to arrange what at that moment could only have been an armed forces' victory. On the basis of hindsight, it is easy to accuse the ambassador of misjudgment. It would be nearer the truth to consider him a victim of bad luck. No one could have foreseen that the conflict would take another sharp turn in the next twenty-four hours and transmute his refusal to mediate into the surpassing irony of the entire crisis.

A fully satisfactory account of what happened on the evening of April 27 and morning of April 28 to change the perspective from a collapse of the rebels to a collapse of the armed forces does not yet seem available. The official U.S. interpretation, as expressed by the President on May 2, is that the collapse of Colonel Caamaño's forces on April 27 enabled the Communists to move in and take over and really seize and place into their hands the originally popular democratic revolution. The implication is that the Communists defeated the armed forces and revived the revolt under their own leadership. On the other hand, it is known that Colonel Caamaño, Colonel Montes Arache, and others of their group, infuriated by what they considered Ambassador Bennett's insulting behavior in rejecting their request for mediation, went back to the Duarte bridge and renewed their resistance to the incursion of General Wessin's tank force. It should be kept in mind that over 1,000 officers and enlisted men fought with Colonel Caamaño to the bitter end.

Other U.S. sources suggest that Colonel Caamaño, now in charge of the revolt, again benefited from cross purposes within the Dominican armed forces. The testimony before Senator Fulbright's committee led him to comment: "Owing to a degree of disorganization and timidity on the part of the anti-rebel forces which no one, including the U.S. Embassy and the rebels themselves, anticipated, the rebels were still fighting on the morning of Wednesday, April 28."* And Representative Armistead I. Selden, Jr. of Alabama, chairman of the House Sub-committee on Inter-American Affairs, and as such also privy to all the documentation, attributed the rebel recovery on April 28 at least in part to

---

* *Congressional Record*, Senate, September 15, 1965, pp. 23001-01.

the fact that "the armed forces under command of Gen. Wessin y Wessin did not move" and "the Dominican Army was sitting out at San Isidro base doing nothing." * Whenever the armed forces met much resistance, it appears, many of the soldiers lost their taste for fighting and deserted *en masse*. The problem may well be why the overwhelmingly superior Dominican army did not fight harder rather than why their opponents were able to fight so well.

Thus a number of factors other than the alleged Communist push and takeover may explain the armed forces' reversal on April 28. It is certainly reasonable to suppose that Colonel Caamaño did not administer any political tests to anyone who was willing to go out and fight in the darkest hours of April 27-28. But the theory of the Communist "miracle" was never very convincing. If the Communists, with nothing more than Molotov cocktails, some machine-guns and small arms at their disposal, could have overwhelmed at minimum an infantry regiment and tanks from San Isidro, another infantry regiment from San Cristóbal, plus the Dominican air force and navy, all in a matter of hours, they would certainly have been strong and headstrong enough to attack the first few hundred marines who landed on April 28-29. The

---

* *Ibid.*, House of Representatives, September 23, 1965, p. 24075.

Communists would have been delighted to exchange them for the Dominican military as their real enemy. One little understands Fidel Castro or the Castroite mentality if one can believe that the Dominican Castroites, flushed with a lightning victory over the entire Dominican military establishment, would have missed a golden opportunity to wage a holy war of "national liberation" against direct U.S. military intervention.

In any event, Ambassador Bennett woke up on Wednesday, April 28, to an altogether different situation. Instead of the Boschists begging him to intercede, the C.I.A.'s brain child, Colonel Benoit's military junta, was crying for help. This unexpected upset again gave the United States an opportunity to demonstrate how it was not "taking sides in the internal struggle" and not "'supporting' either of the factions contending for power."

We may now take a closer look at the two cables from Ambassador Bennett on the afternoon of April 28, which had supposedly convinced President Johnson that he had to send in the marines for no other purpose than to save American lives. We have been solemnly told by the President and the Secretary of State that the first cable at about 3 P.M. had broken the news to them that the Dominican "governmental authorities" could no longer protect Americans—but that it contained no request from the ambassador for U.S. armed intervention. Then at about 5:15 P.M. came the other cable with more or less the same message from the Dominican "law enforcement and military officials" but now accompanied by the ambassador's urgent appeal for immediate troop landings.

The only deduction that can be drawn from this account is that something had happened in the two-and-a-quarter hours between 3 P.M. and 5:15 P.M. to change the ambassador's mind about the necessity for U.S. armed intervention. In subsequent statements, the President tried to give the impression that what had happened was greater personal danger for American citizens, and even for the ambassador himself. "As we talked to Ambassador Bennett," the President related somewhat melodramatically six days later, "he said to apparently one of the girls who brought him a cable, he said, please get away from the window, that glass is going to cut your head, because the glass had been shattered, and we heard the bullets coming through the office where he was sitting while talking to us."* As time passed, the President's saga of the ambassador's ordeal on April 28 became more and more imaginative, until seven weeks later, he had Mr. Bennett "talking to us from under

* *Department of State Bulletin*, May 24, 1965, p. 821.

a desk while bullets were going through his windows." *

One of those who has read Mr. Bennett's second message, Philip Geyelin, was surprised to find that it was not at all as anguished about the safety of Americans as Mr. Johnson had led him to believe. Geyelin wrote:

Though Mr. Johnson, with the poetic license to which a politician may be entitled, was later to report that he received at 5:16 P.M. on Wednesday [April 28] a cable from Ambassador Bennett, warning that "you must land troops immediately or blood will run in the streets, American blood will run in the streets," the actual message was considerably more low-key.

It did recommend the landing of marines and did state, in one short sentence, that the lives of U.S. citizens were endangered. But it dwelt at far greater length on the rapid collapse of the anti-rebel drive and on the pathos of the weary, weeping generals in the "loyalist" headquarters at San Isidro air base. And it contained a revealing passage which for security reasons must be paraphrased. If the policymakers preferred, the embassy said in effect, the troops could be sent in with a mission of covering the evacuation; the clear implication was that the embassy had some other real mission in mind, such as a show of force to hearten the anti-rebel junta.†

115

---

* *Ibid.,* July 5, 1965, p. 20.
† *The Wall Street Journal,* June 25, 1965.

There is also some question about the veri-similitude of the details with which the President embellished his telephone conversation with the ambassador (which apparently took place after the arrival of the second cable).* Tad Szulc looked into the circumstances and found:

There was intermittent sniper fire, apparently by irregulars or plain hoodlums, around the embassy when Mr. Bennett spoke to the President. Somehow the idea was conveyed to the President that the embassy was at that moment under direct heavy machine-gun fire. As Mr. Johnson later related the episode, Mr. Bennett and his secretary were under their desks as the ambassador spoke to the White House.

But embassy officials said later that at no time had the embassy building been fired upon by machine guns. For that matter, despite many subsequent sniper firings, there were never any bullet marks on the embassy's walls.

If danger to Americans was the controlling

*Senator George A. Smathers said that it occurred during the President's consultation with congressional leaders after the decision to send in the marines had been made (*Congressional Record*, Senate, September 15, 1965, p. 23007). Thus the decision had had nothing to do with these sound effects. Senator Stephen M. Young of Ohio later tried to explain away the under-the-desk story as a "theatrical touch" for which the President should not be blamed inasmuch as he was relying on the ambassador's statements (*ibid.*, September 22, 1965, p. 23846).

factor, there was no good reason why Ambassador Bennett should have made up his mind between about 3 P.M. and about 5:15 P.M. No less dangerous fighting in the streets and around the embassy had raged intermittently for at least three days, and the single most explosive incident had occurred the day before at the Hotel Embajador without having caused him to lose his aplomb. By conjuring up such a vivid scene of an ambassador who advised him to send in the marines while crouched under a desk ducking bullets flying through his office, the President inadvertently encouraged the impression that Mr. Bennett may have temporarily surrendered to a panicky concern for his own and other Americans' safety. On the contrary, the ambassador had something else on his mind, and he never made any attempt to disguise it.

Oddly, too, President Johnson referred to the Benoit junta as the Dominican Republic's "governmental authorities." Colonel Benoit merely signed the messages as "President of the Military Junta of the Government of the Dominican Republic." The headquarters of the junta was the San Isidro air base. When Reid Cabral resigned and the United States refused to recognize the provisional government of Molina Ureña, the Dominican Republic was literally left without any "governmental authorities." The Benoit junta was a self-appointed body which merely represented the armed forces behind it. It had been in existence no more than a few hours when it was forced to appeal for help.

By referring to the junta as "governmental authorities," President Johnson conferred on it a degree of recognition which it had in no way earned in law or in fact. The President's curious slip may have been necessary in order to give his order to the Marines a semblance of formal legitimacy that it would otherwise have lacked. Nevertheless, it may also have betrayed an implicit assumption on the part of the U.S. government that the Benoit junta should be treated as if it were the Dominican "government" of the moment. Authorities on international law may well marvel at this junta which was set up "at the instance" of a U.S. intelligence agency and, after a few hours of existence, was accepted as the Dominican "governmental authorities" just as it was obliged to confess that it had lost all authority.

The plot thickens if we turn our attention to what the Dominican "governmental authorities" had told Mr. Bennett that had impelled him to send these two cables. Fortunately, we have the text of what is supposed to have been the key message from Colonel Benoit to Ambassador Bennett. It reads:

> Regarding my earlier request I wish to add that American lives are in danger and conditions of public disorder make it impossible to provide adequate protection. I therefore ask

you for temporary intervention and assistance in restoring order in this country.*

The reader will note a telltale phrase at the beginning of this message—"Regarding my earlier request." In effect, Colonel Benoit had sent two messages, but only one has been made public. The missing message is also the missing link in the chain of events that we have been trying to unravel.

We still do not have the text of Colonel Benoit's first message but we have two very authoritative versions from members of the Senate Foreign Relations Committee of what it conveyed. Senator Fulbright tells us:

> In mid-afternoon of April 28, Col. Pedro Bartolomé Benoit, head of a junta which had been hastily assembled, asked again, this time in writing, for U.S. troops on the ground that this was the only way to prevent a Communist takeover; no mention was made of the junta's inability to protect American lives.†

Senator Clark read the same meaning into Colonel Benoit's first message:

> That junta sent word to Ambassador Bennett, "You had better send American troops in because a Communist takeover threatens."**

119

---

* This note was first made public on May 7, 1965, in the report of the first O.A.S. investigating committee.

† *Congressional Record*, Senate, September 15, 1965, p. 23001.

** *Ibid.*, September 17, 1965, p. 23366.

The forthrightness of this request was not what the ambassador had bargained for. At this juncture on April 28, the evidence in Washington of a Communist takeover was virtually nonexistent. So Colonel Benoit was instructed what to say in order to get the U.S. troops that he wanted.

Here, according to Senator Fulbright, is what happened next:

> This request was denied in Washington, and Benoit was thereupon told that the United States would not intervene unless he said he could not protect American citizens present in the Dominican Republic. Benoit was thus told in effect that if he said American lives were in danger, the United States would intervene. And that is precisely what happened.

Senator Clark, as usual, gives us a more colloquial account of what took place:

> Ambassador Bennett sent word back, "I can't get away with bringing Americans in on that ground because the evidence is not clear. If you will change your request and make it in writing, and ask American forces to intervene in order to protect American lives, then I believe that we can persuade Washington to do it."

So Benoit changed his position and put it on the basis of protecting American lives. Bennett forwarded that post haste to the State Department and to the White House, and troops were sent in.

Senator Wayne L. Morse of Oregon, another member of the same committee, related:

> What Secretary Mann and Secretary of State Rusk have failed to tell the American people is that our Ambassador to the Dominican Republic had urged the police authorities to make such a request for intervention so that American assistance could be justified and could be obtained to thwart the rebels. That is the kind of collusion which existed between the American Ambassador to the Dominican Republic and the military junta which had imposed tyranny upon the Dominican people who were rising up in revolution against the junta and also against American aid to that junta.*

In effect, Ambassador Bennett first put words into Colonel Benoit's mouth or pen, and then used those words to justify sending in U.S. troops. The rest of the operation in Washington was mainly an effort to cover up the tracks of this rather extraordinary transaction. In a totalitarian country, it would probably have taken years, if not decades, to uncover these tracks. In a free country, it took only a few weeks or months. Senator Fulbright told nothing but the unwanted and unvarnished truth in his speech of September 15, which was informed with a grandeur and integrity that can hardly be matched in recent congressional history:

121

---

* *Congressional Record,* Senate, October 15, 1965, p. 26185.

'The United States intervened in the Dominican Republic for the purpose of preventing the victory of a revolutionary force which was judged to be Communist dominated. On the basis of Ambassador Bennett's messages to Washington, there is no doubt that the threat of Communism rather than danger to American lives was his primary reason for recommending military intervention.

One may settle, then, for a minimal interpretation of the Johnson-Mann-Bennett policy. If it was not aimed at obtaining victory for the reactionary military forces, it certainly did not wish to see them lose. Conversely, if it did not do anything to defeat the revolt, it was willing to do almost anything to prevent its success.

This policy also managed to prolong the civil war for the second time certainly and the third time possibly in four days. The fighting might never have flared up but for the putative pressure of the military attachés on April 24 and 25; the revolt would have lost its outstanding military and civilian leaders if Ambassador Bennett had agreed to help them give up on April 27; and only twenty-four hours later, the complete collapse of the other side was admittedly averted by sending in U.S. troops. Fate and a word have rarely played such tricks on a diplomat as befell Mr. Bennett on April 27 and 28; in the name of "non-intervention," he missed an opportunity to end the conflict successfully for "his" side, and then he non-intervened U.S. marines and paratroops right into a shooting civil war.

The walkie-talkies and the non-intervention of the U.S. marines on April 28 do not constitute the only evidence of how the United States "refrained," during the first violent days, from supporting either of the "factions" struggling for power.

I have previously mentioned the unintentional eavesdropping of U.S. correspondents aboard the *Boxer* as they approached Santo Domingo on Thursday morning, April 29. To their astonishment, they were able to hear official U.S. communications through both a transistor radio and the ship's radio, evidently because the embassy's messages were being relayed to the San Isidro base via the aircraft carrier. Even more disconcerting was the discovery that the ambassador of their nation which, as far as they still knew, was fiercely protesting its neutrality, was manifestly encouraging and assisting the San Isidro generals. They heard lengthy exchanges about the delivery of U.S. equipment and food to the San Isidro forces. Kurzman and Szulc cite almost the same words in one message from Ambassador Bennett to Colonel Benoit: ". . . Do you need more aid?. . . Believe that with determination your plans will succeed." Szulc adds that a correspondent asked the ambassa-

123

dor later that day about the radio conversations which had provided the newsmen with their first inkling that something untoward was going on.

"The ambassador looked embarrassed and changed the subject," Szulc notes.*

---

* A Dominican, Dr. Pedro Manuel Casals Victoria, founder and General Secretary of the Democratic Socialist Party, says that he also listened in on these messages. Dr. Casals has written: "But the Ambassador from Georgia, to whom our triumph appeared inconceivable and who saw possibly his career, his proposals and perhaps his instructions rolled into the ground in the face of the popular victory, ordered Wessin to resist and even to make another small attack before the bulk of the North American troops arrived to occupy the San Isidro base. Constitutionalist forces listened to his communications through the Embassy's transmitter, and I personally monitored his communications with the Consulate of Santiago offering to send troops and overheard other communications between the commanders of the 2nd Division, the North American base of Ramey Field in Puerto Rico and the Embassy in Santo Domingo" (*New America*, July 25, 1965). It should be noted that Dr. Casals was Minister of Finance in the first post-Bosch government; he resigned, after three months, in protest against the governmental corruption which he was unable to stop.

11

ON THIS SAME DAY, APRIL 29, TWO OTHER leading characters in the Dominican drama, General Antonio Imbert Barrera and former U.S. Ambassador John Bartlow Martin, moved to the center of the stage. As the *Boxer's* helicopters landed the first group of correspondents in Santo Domingo, they spotted Imbert, accompanied by a U.S. colonel and a Dominican bishop, getting into another helicopter, obviously on their way to the *Boxer*. Late that night, Mr. Martin received a telephone call from President Johnson's special assistant, Bill D. Moyers, to come to Washington to consult on the Dominican crisis.

Martin returned to Santo Domingo the next evening, April 30, and one of the first persons he went to see was Antonio Imbert Barrera. Imbert reminds one of the former Cuban strongman, Fulgencio Batista. The two built up their political careers on their association with the military but were not themselves military men; Batista had been an army stenographer and Imbert was given the honorary rank of Brigadier General at the end of 1962. What a U.S. official told Philip Geyelin about Imbert might well have been said about Batista: "Tony Imbert is a hood—but with all the advantages of a hood."* Like Batista, too, Imbert was perfectly capable of working with anyone who happened to serve his interests. Trujillo had once appointed Imbert a provincial governor, and he was one of the two surviving assassins of Trujillo; the Communists had also made themselves useful to Imbert in return for his favors, and now he was making his bid for power to save the country from Communism.†

As Mr. Martin told the story in *Life* of May 28, he visited Imbert again at the latter's invitation on May 3. "Various people" had asked him to "reconstitute" the three-man military junta headed by Colonel Benoit, Imbert said. He was, they had told him, the only man in the Dominican Republic "strong enough" to force the "old generals" to leave the country. Then ensued this dialogue:

126

---

* *Wall Street Journal*, June 30, 1965.

† For Imbert's dealings with the Communists in 1962, see Virginia Prewett, the Washington *Daily News*, June 16, 1965, and Norman Gall, the Washington *Post*, June 17, 1965. Both articles are based on depositions by Imbert's go-betweens, the originals of which I have seen. The stories seem entirely in character with the man.

I [Martin] asked, "Do you want to do it?"

He said, "I do it. For my country. Not for myself. Whatta hell I want to get into this mess for? I can sit here quiet."

I said, "We are not going to support any military dictatorship."

"I know."

"And I don't think any better of the old generals than you do. Can you get rid of them?"

"I fix."

"What about the junta,"

"We leave one of them in, Colonel Benoit. The others resign."

"Will they?"

"Su-u-re," drawing it out, a way he has.

"What kind of a government is this going to be? Who'll be in it?"

"No politicians, you can be sure of that Mr. Martin."

And, as far as the readers of *Life* could know, this is how Antonio Imbert applied for the job of forming and heading another junta.* The man who had gotten into the mess of assassinating Trujillo, who had gotten into the mess of the post-Trujillo Council of State as

---

* On another occasion, Mr. Martin explicitly stated that he was personally responsible for giving Imbert the green light. Here is some of the dialogue on the CBS program, "Santo Domingo—Why Are We There?" of May 13, 1965:

Marvin Kalb: Mr. Martin, the question comes up, why General Imbert? Did we find him, or did he find us?

John Bartlow Martin: He found us, specifically me.

Kalb: What happened?

Martin: Well, he called me and asked me to come

one of its seven members, which had been one of the chief impresarios of the mess that had resulted in the anti-Bosch coup, who had made the mess of the Dominican police his private preserve, had been reluctantly talked into the mess of taking power in May 1965—for his country, not for himself. The old fixer knew in advance who in the existing three-man junta had to stay and who could be counted on to go. He accepted three civilian figureheads who were never heard from again. He was so incorrigibly venal that he did not scruple to betray his former comrades-in-arms. For part of the deal to make Imbert the top man required the expulsion from the country of a number of leading military commanders to give Imbert's junta a new look. Thus, General Belisário Peguero, whom Imbert had put in charge of the police and whom Reid Cabral had fired in one of the reforms that had brought about his downfall, General Montás Guerrero, who had belatedly brought his San Cristóbal regiment into the capital, General Atila Luna Pérez of the air force, who had worked with Imbert on the

and see him. And he told me that he had been approached by a number of Dominicans. He told them that they could not support either the rebel government or the San Isidro junta, which represented the military elements that the rebellion had begun against. These people, the Dominicans, had asked Imbert to form a third force, a new government. And I told him, "Go ahead."

anti-Bosch coup, and three or four others were unceremoniously hustled out of the country.* To his credit, it must be said that General Wessin refused to play this game, and a resignation already announced, was repudiated by him.†

Mr. Martin writes as if he had so much authority that he could tell Imbert to go

---

* General Wessin testified before the Senate Internal Security Subcommittee on October 1, 1965, that he was visited by Ambassador Bennett and U.S. commander Lt. Gen. Bruce Palmer, Jr., in the first week of May. Ambassador Bennett allegedly told him that he would "have to leave" the Dominican Republic in order to permit the country to "return to normal." General Wessin says that he asked why other officers were not also ordered to leave, and he later sent Mr. Bennett a handwritten letter suggesting the removal of Generals Montás Guerrero, Atila Luna Pérez, Félix Hermida, Rivera Cuesta, and Commodore Julio Rib Santamaría because they had agreed with the rebels at the outset and had later changed their minds and because he considered them to be "corrupt" (pp. 162-64). General Wessin named only these five officers, but the list handed to General Imbert by Ambassador Bennett seems to have contained three additional generals: Manuel A. García Urbáez, Renato Hungría Morell and Peguero Guerrero. Commodore Rib Santamaría had already left the Dominican Republic some time previously (¡Ahora!, May 16, 1965, p. 14).

†General Wessin claims that he agreed to leave the country only after the situation had returned to normal and after a reasonable period but that the Ambassador had misunderstood him. Mr. Bennett undoubtedly thought that the removal of the officers named by Wessin was the price for the latter's own departure.

ahead. Whether or not he should have given a little more credit to Ambassador Bennett and the C.I.A., there is no doubt that General Imbert succeeded Colonel Benoit as the chosen instrument of U.S. policy. On May 26, Secretary of State Rusk blandly told a news conference: "As far as the civilian-military group under General Imbert's leadership is concerned, we did encourage them to form a group that could try to assure the normal processes of the countryside which was not involved in downtown Santo Domingo." He reiterated: "And so we did encourage these gentlemen to associate themselves and to try to help deal with the problems of those areas of the country that were not directly involved in the violence in Santo Domingo itself." From these words, one might gather that Imbert was "encouraged" merely to form a "group" to "help" (whom?) to deal with (what?) problems outside the capital. In fact, Imbert set up what he called a "Government of National Reconstruction," which Mr. Martin says "began to behave surprisingly like a government." Since by the time Mr. Rusk spoke, it had already appointed a foreign minister and representatives to the United Nations and the O.A.S., and demanded all the rights and privileges accorded to legitimate governments, it is difficult to understand the Secretary's language. One can hardly recall a Secretary of State afflicted with such squeamishness.

Mr. Rusk also cast some doubt on Mr. Martin's credentials. When he was asked to comment on the "ethical question" of Mr. Martin's kiss-and-tell article, the Secretary of State delivered himself as follows: "Mr. Martin was not down there on an official appointment. He was not down there as a salaried employee of the Government." What was he down there for? Only "to establish contact" with people he had known as ambassador during Bosch's administration. His status had only been that of a "private citizen" to assist Ambassador Bennett. We were asked to believe, then, that two "private citizens," John Bartlow Martin and Antonio Imbert Barreras, had had a private little conversation out of which had come a "group" which had surprisingly behaved like a government.

No one, of course, was deceived, least of all the forces behind the new junta. Only a week later, when the Bundy mission seemed to be pulling the rug from under it, Imbert's chief of staff, General Jacinto Martínez Araña, protested: "We cannot stop because the present government was selected, you know, by a group of American people, United States people. One of them is the ambassador and some more, you know."* And Hal Hendrix, from Imbert's corner, reported heartlessly: "Exactly

*General Martínez Araña on the CBS program, "Santo Domingo—Why Are We There?" May 31, 1965.

a week earlier American representatives here had stage-managed the creation of a five-member military-civilian junta government of national reconstruction" (New York *World-Telegram and Sun,* May 18, 1965). Indeed, if Mr. Bundy had had his way at this time, American representatives would have been able to take credit for having stage-managed the creation of Dominican juntas at the rate of one every ten days.*

---

*I have chosen here to ignore the deleterious effects on the revolt of the strictly military action by the U.S. force. It cut the rebel zone in two and later permitted the regrouped pro-Imbert troops to wipe out the northern rebel-held sector. Inasmuch as I am not trying to deal with every phase of the revolt, and the military actions raise a whole set of different problems, I have limited myself to behind-the-scenes political actions and decisions which go directly to the heart of U.S. policy.

12

OF ALL THE CONTROVERSIAL ISSUES THAT AROSE
in the course of the Dominican crisis, the
least necessary to dispute is President Johnson's pronouncement that there was a Communist takeover of the revolt.

The trouble starts as soon as one asks when
the Communist takeover took place. One
school of U.S. officials, as we have seen, inspired stories to the effect that Bosch had sold
out to the Communists before the revolt. One
of the State Department's advocates, Adolf A.
Berle, assured readers of *The Reporter* of
May 20, 1965 that the pro-Bosch forces had
been "infiltrated and then dominated by the
trained Communist elements" within 48 hours,
that is, by April 26. Mr. Berle evidently knew
better than the President, who dated the takeover from the temporary Boschist setback on
April 27.

Privately, of course, Bennett was indoctrinating Washington to the effect that the conflict was one between Castroism and anti-Castroism by, at latest, the afternoon of April 28. After the marines had landed at about 7 P.M. that evening, Mr. Bennett was evidently afraid that their mission might indeed be limited to protecting Americans, and he went all-out to prevent that unpleasant eventuality. At 8 P.M., he sent what Szulc thinks may have been the most crucial single recommendation from the embassy in the entire crisis: "I recommend that serious thought be given to armed intervention to restore order beyond a mere protection of livês. If the present loyalist efforts fail, the power will go to groups whose aims are identical with those of the Communist Party. We might have to intervene to prevent another Cuba." And in the famous or notorious briefing of April 29, Mr. Bennett handed out the first list of 53 Communist names.

In any event, Ambassador Bennett did not yet commit himself publicly to the Communist takeover. Mr. Bennett permitted "private citizen" John Bartlow Martin to make the first U.S. announcement that the revolution was Communist-controlled at a joint press conference in the embassy on May 2. Martin is quoted as having said: "This was originally a PRD attempt to restore Bosch's constitutional government, but I am now convinced after having talked to many people on the rebel side that this is Communist-dominated, and moderate elements of the PRD are themselves aware of this fact."* He had already sent this advice to the President who that same day went on record in support of the extreme Communist-takeover line.

Previously I raised the question why the President was far more cautious and tentative about the Communist takeover on April 30 than on May 2. The answer very likely lies in Mr. Martin's role during those three days. An open enemy of Juan Bosch could not have done what a self-professed friend did. This Brutus-like stab inflicted more harm on Bosch's cause than all Wessin's soldiers were able to do.

In his book, *Overtaken by Events*, published in 1966, Mr. Martin added little in his effort to make a convincing case for the "Communist takeover" to what he had written in *Life* and what U.S. official agencies had already tried to foist on public opinion. But he made two general observations which cast unexpected light on his practical decisions.

---

* This is Szulc's version. Kurzman quotes Martin as having said that the revolution had "fallen under the domination of Castro Communists" and "they are now in control." In his *Life* article, Mr. Martin alludes to the fact that "I had said publicly that in my judgment his [Bosch's] party had fallen under the domination of adventurers and Castro-Communists." The latter version goes much farther than merely saying that the revolt had fallen under Communist domination, for it specifically refers to Bosch's *party*.

The first one comes after Mr. Martin describes how the United States committed itself to General Imbert, whom he calls a "political primitive" who "did not understand ideas," and then tossed him aside. Martin writes: "I thought: This is the second time I have betrayed my Dominican friends. First the rebels; now Imbert." A harsher verdict on Martin's role—he is candid enough not to put "betrayed" in quotation marks—would be hard to imagine.

Martin's other observation is even more revealing. As he rightly notes, a political structure" collapsed in the Dominican Republic on April 24, 1965. It collapsed, he feels, for many different reasons—"Boschist idealism, revenge, plunder, Communist directive, anti-Reid, anti-corruption, sheer adventure and excitement, the highest ideals of liberalism and the meanest effort to pick a winner." Once the masses were swept into the struggle, however, he argues that only the Communists could benefit from it. "Men and women like this," he asserts, "have nowhere to go except to the Communists. All other doors are shut." And again, he theorizes, "It is not names of Communists, or numbers, that is important. It is the process itself—the fusion of the blood-bath."

From this point of view, there is no need to find out who and how many the Dominican

Communists were that took over the revolt in such short order. The "process" was enough to do the job for them. With such a theory of popular revolution, it is small wonder that Martin quickly lost his bearings in the confused Dominican outburst.

For about a week after John Bartlow Martin and President Johnson made the first U.S. statements committing this country to the idea of a Communist takeover of the revolt, it became the U.S. party line, though different and somewhat more equivocal expressions were also used. On May 3, Adlai Stevenson was instructed to say at the U.N. that "Communist leaders, many of them trained in Cuba, have taken increasing control of what was initially a democratic movement." On May 4, the President declared that "some 58 Communists began to rise on that crock of milk, they came to the surface and took increased leadership in the movement and the leaders and friends of ex-President Bosch were more or less shoved in the background and stepped aside." On May 8, Secretary of State Rusk told John Hightower of the Associated Press that the U.S. government had acted on mounting evidence that "the Communists had captured the revolution according to plan." And on May 9, in the New York *Times* interview with Max Frankel, Under Secretary Mann said that the democratic revolution had "moved into the hands of a band of Communist agents."

But then a strange thing happened. U.S. spokesmen began to back away from this extreme position and to cast doubt that the Communists had really succeeded in taking over the revolt. For example, at his news conference on May 26, Secretary Rusk merely talked of a "possibility" and "a very serious threat" that Communists would seize control of armed mobs. On June 9, Leonard C. Meeker, the State Department's Legal Adviser, delivered an address before the Foreign Law Association in which he would go no further than to allege that there had been "a grave risk" and a very real "threat" and an appearance that the Communists had been "in a fair way" to take over. Most curiously of all, in Atlanta, Georgia, on September 17, Ambassador Bennett himself praised U.S. policy in the Dominican Republic in the following terms: "The Communists were prevented from taking over in a chaotic situation and pushing aside the democratic elements involved in the revolt." These words must represent the most astonishing repudiation of President Johnson's position on record, for they clearly implied that the Communists had never taken over and really seized and placed their hands on the popular democratic revolution of April 24.

And thus we came full circle. First the United States sent in the marines because the Communists had taken over the revolt, and then the United States claimed credit for having prevented the Communists from taking over the revolt. In fact, the congressional defenders of the administration's policy argued that the intervention was justified on the basis of the "risk" and "threat" and "possibility" of a Communist takeover, not the accomplished fact.

If we accept something that Under Secretary Mann told Max Frankel, however, there is no longer any need to argue about the original U.S. justification for its military intervention. This is what Mr. Mann said: "But there really is no problem, as far as our policy is concerned, unless and until the Communists succeed in actually capturing and controlling a movement."

By this criterion, a "risk," "threat," or "possibility" is not good enough. That is possibly why President Johnson went as far as he did on May 2, but U.S. spokesmen subsequently moved further and further away from that dangerously exposed position to one more easily defensible.

This strategic retreat may also be observed in the strange fate of the various "lists" of Dominican Communists and Castroites.

By chance, the new director of the C.I.A.,

Admiral William F. Raborn, Jr.. was sworn in on April 28, a few hours before President Johnson ordered the marines to land. At least as late as April 28, according to Senator Clark, Raborn was able to produce the names of only three Communists allegedly implicated in the revolt.* From 3 P.M. to 7 P.M. on April 28, President Johnson disclosed on May 4, U.S. intelligence indicated that no more than two of the "prime leaders in the rebel forces" were men "with a long history of Communist association and insurrections," one of whom had allegedly fought in the Spanish civil war. Later reports, the President also said, brought the figure up to eight. Then special "alerts" were sent out for more names. On April 29, as we have seen, Ambassador Bennett upped the ante to 53. This jump was apparently made possible by ransacking old, pre-revolt lists for Dominicans who had been previously reported active in Communist movements. For this reason, the first lists were curiously dated, with much of the data no more recent than 1963. On May 1, a list of 54 was leaked to the press in Washington. By May 3, according to the President, he had "the names and addresses and experience and numbers and background" of 58. When four of these proved to be dupli-

140

---

*Congressional Record, Senate, September 17, 1965, p. 23366. Senator Clark did not give the exact date for the three but said that they had been produced 72 hours before the 58.

cations, only 54 were published in the New York *Times* of May 6.* And in mid-June a final list of 77 was released *sub rosa* in Washington.†

One thing is immediately apparent about these lists. They were all *ex post facto* jobs, hastily put together to justify an already adopted policy rather than to provide raw material for a policy in gestation. Whatever may have been right or wrong about the lists, they were not available to President Johnson and his small circle of advisers when they had to make up their minds to send the marines to frustrate a reported Communist takeover. In fact, if we may judge from the list published in the New York *Times* on May 6, the President still did not have much to go by. Only one person on it was allegedly "involved in the direction of the insurrection," and only one other was classified as a "probable military leader." Of the 54, only 20 were positively identified as having taken part in the April 1965 revolt. One entry simply reads: "Pro-Castro student leader." Even the list of 77 a month later contains only six imputed to be in "the top leadership group of government."

141

---

* An early edition carried 55 names but, owing to a duplication, the number was reduced to 54 in the later edition.

† This list may be found in the *Congressional Record*, House, September 23, 1965, pp. 24079-81.

In fact, we have at least one authoritative testimonial that, on April 28, the President was able to give assurances not that there was a preponderant Communist influence but only a "definite" one. On that day, before taking action, Mr. Johnson telephoned Senator Richard B. Russell of Georgia, who was then at home. Mr. Russell later told the Senate:

> The President was kind enough to ask me what I thought of the situation. I asked him if there were any indications of a definite Communist influence in the so-called rebel forces. He stated that there was little doubt that there was a definite Communist influence there, and I told him that, in my opinion, he had no alternative other than to proceed to send the Armed Forces to Santo Domingo to avoid another Cuba. *

It is possible to argue that the President was later proven right by the information which the intelligence agencies subsequently gathered. But if we are also interested in what the President had before him at the moment of decision, we can hardly fail to be impressed by the paucity of the data.

142

The trouble with these lists was that they tended to prove that the Communists had organized their own groups headed by Communists, not that they controlled the far more nu-

---

*Congressional Record, Senate, September 21, 1965, p., 23667.

merous non-Communist groups or the rebellion as a whole. With the two exceptions already noted, the list of 54 merely ascribed such activities to those on it as "armed for action," "making Molotov cocktails," and "distributing leaflets." It was notably weak at the crucial point—whether the Communists had gained control of the rebel leadership. The correspondents to whom Ambassador Bennett gave his list of 53 spotted this weakness immediately, even before they discovered other reasons to find fault with it. The only substantial tie-up between the Communists and Colonel Caamaño at this time was made in a charge that he had appointed "three men of well-established Communist sympathies and associations" to posts in his "provisional government." On investigation, the correspondents soon learned (a) that they were almost certainly not Communists, and (b) that Caamaño had not appointed them to any cabinet posts. When Kurzman pointed out these blemishes to an embassy official, the latter agreed that a mistake had been made.* As we have seen, the charge that

143

---

* The best treatment of this mix-up is in Kurzman's book, pp. 197-98. The original charges against the three appeared in the New York *Times* story on May 6, 1965. Unfortunately, no one told Senator Frank J. Lausche of Ohio that he no longer had to worry about them. More than four months later, Mr. Lausche rose in the Senate and indignantly proclaimed that "the most ardent Communist of the

Colonel Caamaño had made a deal with Communist leaders on May 4 similarly boomeranged.

By this time, the correspondents in Santo Domingo were so suspicious that they were primed to pounce on every defect in the ambassador's list. James Nelson Goodsell of the *Christian Science Monitor* gave it the most thorough going-over. "A good degree of sloppy intelligence work went into the preparation of the lists," was his verdict on May 19, 1965, "for they contain the names of persons in prison at the time of the April 24 revolt, others out of the country at that time, and still others who are not Communists but rather are widely known as Nationalists who agree with Communists on the anti-American issue." Goodsell found two in prison; six not in the county; four jailed within two days of the

whole group" had been put in charge of the "investigative forces" of a "temporary government" formed in April (*Congressional Record*, Senate, September 17, 1965, p. 23345). The Senator was referring to Luis Hómero Lajara Burgos, who had been appointed Director General of Security in the two-day Molina Ureña provisional government but had not been reappointed by Colonel Caamaño. Sr. Lajara Burgos had also been a Rear Admiral (ret.) and Chief of Staff of the Dominican Navy, Chief of the Dominican National Police, member of the General Staff of the Inter-American Defense Board, and Naval Attaché, Dominican Embassy, Washington, D.C. Norman Thomas including a contribution by Luis Hómero Lajara Burgos in the pamphlet, *Dominican Republic: A Study in the New Imperialism*. Kurzman writes of Lajara Burgos: "A naval officer, he was, I found, regarded even by conservative Dominicans as anti-Communist."

outbreak and, therefore, *hors de combat* when the Communist takeover supposedly took place; at least three others released from jail before the list was promulgated; four and possibly six not in Santo Domingo at the time. If Goodsell was right, from 19 to 21, or almost 40 per cent of the list, could not have played active roles at the time it was issued. This percentage of error may have been too great, but the list-makers themselves admitted to a margin of error of almost 20 per cent. When the list of 77 was given out, 10 of those on the original list of 54 had been removed from it.

Goodsell, of course, was not the only enterprising correspondent who refused to take the lists on faith. Mauro Calamandrei of *L'Espresso* (Rome) and Luis Suárez of *Siempre* (Mexico City) went looking for the redoubtable Manuel González y González, whom President Johnson himself had mentioned as a veteran of the Spanish civil war. Calamandrei had no trouble locating him several times at home, and Suárez talked to him in the street, a pistol in his belt as he fixed a jammed gun for a young rebel fighter. But he hardly impressed them as "the probable military leader in the current insurrection"; the revolt had caught him by surprise as much as anyone else, as he was seeing off an aunt on a trip; he had never met Colonel Caamaño; and it was his father who had fought in the Spanish civil war when he was still in his teens.

The skepticism of the *Christian Science*

145

Monitor was bad enough. But who would have expected to find these blasphemous words in the *Wall Street Journal* of June 25: "What the record also suggests is a some-times-carefree, sometimes-clumsy tendency toward inconsistency, contradiction and even outright misrepresentation for the sake of ex-pediency?"*

It is not often that journalists can be said to have saved the honor of their country. This was, I believe, one of those very rare occasions. Tad Szulc, Barnard L. Collier, Dan Kurzman, James Nelson Goodsell, Philip Geyelin, Bert Quint of CBS, and others, made one feel proud of and grateful for a free press without which the moral and political disaster would have been infinitely greater. When they were struggling against the greatest odds to get the truth and make it known, no public figure was able or willing to speak out against the inconsistencies, contradictions, and out-right misrepresentations. In this Dominican crisis, the best and worst of American journal-ism were manifested—but the worst is far less a stranger than the best.

146

---

* Later, Szulc, Collier, and Kurzman became the favorite whipping boys of pro-administration con-gressmen. For some reason, Goodsell and Geyelin did not receive the same treatment, possibly because the very names of their papers might have caused some wonderment, though there is very little of importance in the first three that cannot be found in the last two.

It should be remembered that Ambassador Bennett's list of 53 was issued at the same press conference on April 29 at which he regaled the correspondents with a collection of anti-Caamaño atrocity stories. There was no reason why the sources for his list should have been much better than the sources for his stories. Both were quite clearly the products of hastily enlisted informers and material obtained from the Dominican police and military "intelligence" factories. I do not mean to become indignant about the practice of using informers by all intelligence agencies, but anyone who has had any experience with this type of information, especially in the heat of an unexpected civil war, knows how treacherous it can be. The informers did very badly tipping off the embassy about the imminence of the revolt; they did very badly with the horror tales; they did very badly with the three alleged Communists in Colonel Caamaño's provisional government; and they lived up to their record in the matter of the first lists. Ambassador Bennett later told Al Burt, Latin American editor of the Miami *Herald* (August 22, 1965), that "we had to operate by antenna and by guess." We can sympathize with Mr. Bennett's plight and respect his candor, but that is not how the matter was originally presented to the American people or the world at large, and too much hinged on his antenna and guesswork.

As for John Bartlow Martin's judgment, it was perhaps the most depressing aspect of this whole calamitous affair. As the ambassador to Bosch's government, of whom Bosch had written that he and the Alliance for Progress director, Newell F. Williams, "did not appear to be agents of the U.S. government but rather two Dominicans as anxious as the best of Dominicans to accomplish the impossible for us,"* Mr. Martin was the living symbol of U.S. faith in democracy and social justice, whatever his diplomatic abilities may have been. If there came a time when the U.S. would need to change its policy from what W. Tapley Bennett, Jr. symbolized, Martin would have been an invaluable asset in making it. Instead, he was yanked from home in Connecticut, ulcers and all, to "assist" Mr. Bennett, "open up contact" with the hitherto despised and ignored rebels, and advise the President. He says that he was at first skeptical of reports that the revolt was Communist-led. Only two days later, he was so sure of it that he gave the President the final shove to go overboard on the Communist issue.

In his *Life* article, Mr. Martin set out to

148

---

*Juan Bosch, *Crisis de la Democracia de América en la República Dominicana* (Mexico: Centro de Estudios y Documentación, 1964), p. 155. This book has been issued in an English translation by Praeger (*The Unfinished Experiment*, 239 pp., $5.95).

vindicate this judgment. Presumably he tried to make his case as strong as possible. Yet in the entire article, there are exactly two passages in which the author gives any clue to the basis for his conclusion. In the first, he relates a rather boring interview on May 1 with Colonel Caamaño and his political adviser, Héctor Aristy. As Mr. Martin and his aide, Harry Shlaudeman, departed and got into a car, a crowd gathered and cried, "We trust you, Mr. Martin," and, "We want democracy." But though Mr. Martin tells us compassionately that the crowd was made up of "the Dominican people, the real sufferers—hungry, penniless, disease-ridden, defenseless," he immediately changes his tone and calls it a demonstration that had been "well organized to reinforce our sympathies." Then comes the shocker:

> And Shlaudeman noticed something else: a black-shirted young man, whom he recognized as a member of the Castro-Communist terrorist party, had yelled beside the car, "Yankees go home." Immediately a powerful hand had gripped his shoulder from behind and jerked him away out of sight. He had used the wrong script.

149

I have cited this scene in Mr. Martin's own words because it is literally the only personal experience that he offers to account for his momentous decision. The entire incident turns on a familiar anti-American slogan uttered by a single young man. It might have been the "wrong script" for more than one reason. The young man might have been jerked away because he had been indiscreet or because the owner of the powerful hand did not agree with him—Mr. Martin had no way of knowing. Even if we accept the worst interpretation and consider this shattering little incident a "Communist demonstration," as Mr. Martin seems to do, it still constituted very slight grounds for determining who controlled the entire revolt.

After this, Mr. Martin immediately moves on to May 2 and tells us that he and Shlaudeman "studied the massive evidence assembled by our intelligence agencies" and talked quietly to Dominicans on both sides. From these talks he quotes snatches that are hardly worth repeating. His *pièce de résistance* is really a selection of eleven "dedicated Communists" from Ambassador Bennett's longer list of those who "almost immediately joined the revolt." The most that Mr. Martin says of them is that "our intelligence agents saw many of these men at rebel headquarters and rebel strongholds." What they were seen doing, or what bearing it had on the crucial question of control, deponent doth not say. In any case, Mr. Martin was in no position to evaluate the "massive evidence" put before him, some of which we have already examined. One of his eleven, for example, is Dato

Pagán Perdomo, no doubt a Communist, but hardly capable of almost immediately joining the revolt because he had been safely tucked away in prison at the time.*

On one other point, open to checking, Mr. Martin committed a more serious indiscretion. During a later meeting with Colonel Caamaño, Mr. Martin conveyed the impression that three of the most respected Latin American leaders, who had been called to Washington to advise the President, had inferentially given up the rebel cause for the same reason that Mr. Martin had given it up and, therefore, had decided against coming to Santo Domingo.† This revelation was supposed to break down Colonel Caamaño's resistance to Mr. Martin's viewpoint, and the latter intimates that it hit home: "Caamaño looked shocked" and "Caamaño realized instantly the significance of their decision."

---

* In *Overtaken by Events,* Mr. Martin corrected this blunder in a footnote which reads in part: "Our old friend, Dato Pagán, early reported active in the rebellion, was actually in jail at the time" (p. 673). But Mr. Martin did not have Dato Pagán in jail in his *Life* article, an unwitting confession that he had not been in a position to examine that list of eleven "dedicated Communists" critically.

† This is the only interpretation that I can draw from Mr. Martin's own account. He tells how he was pressing Colonel Caamaño to admit that there were Communists in the rebel leadership. Colonel Caamaño allegedly acknowledged that there were individual Communists around but not in the leadership. Then Mr. Martin comments: "I was far from sure. And I

Colonel Caamaño should have been shocked that Mr. Martin would tell him a cock-and-bull story and then publish it in a national magazine. In *Life* of June 18, 1965, the three Latin American statesmen in question—Rómulo Betancourt, former President of Venezuela, José Figueres, former President of Costa Rica, and Luis Muñoz Marín, former Governor of Puerto Rico—were forced to protest against Mr. Martin's "variance with the truth." They made known that the O.A.S. was responsible for their failure to go to Santo Domingo and that they had at all times been "ready to serve." I do not mean to suggest that Mr. Martin deliberately mislead Colonel Caamaño. I do think that this misunderstanding on his part, and the uses to which he put it, suggest how poorly prepared he was for his difficult assignment.*

I am not sure, however, whether Mr. Mar-

---

think he was, too." This is the prelude to his reference to the three Latin American leaders: "I said, 'I have something to tell you. Time is running out. We have been trying to get Betancourt, Figueres and Muñoz Marín to come here under the O.A.S., but they are not coming.'" This is what reputedly shocked Colonel Caamaño and made him instantly realize the significance of their decision.

* In *Overtaken by Events,* Mr. Martin admits that he may have been wrong, "but what I told Caamaño at the time was what I understood to be the case" (p. 689 note). At this point, however, much hinged on his peculiar misunderstanding, and his indictment of the revolt in *Life* would have been much weakened without it.

tin can be absolved of more serious misrepresentation in his treatment of Juan Bosch. When he saw the Dominican leader in Puerto Rico on May 2 and 3, he had already committed himself publicly to the notion of a Communist takeover of Bosch's movement. After an interval of nineteen months, it was not an auspicious introduction. Instead of making their reunion an effort to reach a new understanding, Mr. Martin was merely bent on persuading Sr. Bosch to accept the U.S. thesis and to support it. To imagine that Sr. Bosch, who had already publicly rejected the thesis and who had been in constant touch with his adherents in Santo Domingo long before Mr. Martin had come on the scene, would be likely to accede to such an appeal was at best naïve. Once Mr. Martin had committed himself openly to the U.S. thesis, he was no longer capable of carrying out that portion of his mission which had envisaged him as the friendly untarnished go-between who might pave the way for better Bosch-U.S. relations. There was no point in sending Mr. Martin to Puerto Rico if he were not going to play a somewhat different role from Mr. Bennett; two Bennetts were hardly an improvement over one.

Even if Mr. Martin's mission to Puerto Rico was doomed, however, his subsequent betrayal of confidence in *Life* was indefensible. He had, after all, been entrusted with an exceedingly delicate diplomatic mission. When his article appeared, things were more confused than ever. Even according to U.S. sources, the Communist tide had receded or was about to recede. and the Boschists were again a force to be reckoned with. Yet Mr. Martin described their leader and his former friend as if he were a blood-crazed psychopath, so incapable of discussing the issues rationally that Mr. Martin "seldom felt more helpless." I cannot recall a diplomatic envoy, whether or not he was technically a "private citizen," who rushed into print with such an indecent breach of good faith. One can only conjecture whether the administration was so anxious to discredit Sr. Bosch that it put him up to it or whether Martin, the journalist, got the better of Martin, the diplomat.

But this is not all. There is reason to believe that the *Life* article committed a far more serious transgression. On this point, we have not only Sr. Bosch's recollection but the word of a man of unquestionable integrity at whose home Mr. Martin and Sr. Bosch met—Chancellor (now President) Jaime Benítez of the University of Puerto Rico. Here is Mr. Martin's version of the discussion on a very controversial point—Sr. Bosch's possible return to Santo Domingo:

> I asked if he himself did not intend to return.
>
> "No," putting up one hand, "I cannot. I am—how do you say it?—burned."

"Would you return to advise and assist in rebuilding the country?"

"No. I cannot. If I return, I am the President."

This seems reasonably clear: Mr. Martin gave Sr. Bosch an opportunity to say that he wanted to return home and the latter categorically refused.

According to Sr. Bosch, this was not at all the case. The subject had actually come up twice. The first time, on the night of May 2, Bosch wrote in the *New Leader* (June 21, 1965), he had asked Martin for a plane to take him to Santo Domingo.

"No, impossible. They'll kill you," he answered.

"But if so many Dominicans are dying, it matters little whether I die," I said.

"Mr. President, you don't understand the situation. Your men, Wessin y Wessin's men, even the Marines have fired at me. The place is in chaos. If you go they will kill you, and you are the leader; you must not die."

This clearly implied that Bosch was willing to return but that Martin tried to dissuade him. Bosch says that the subject came up again the following day. After he had suggested that the constitutional issue might be solved by getting Sr. Molina Ureña out of the Colombian embassy and reinstalling him as provisional president, Mr. Martin telephoned Washington. When he returned, he again asked whether Bosch would return "to advise

155

and assist." This time, Bosch understood that the question of his return was bound up with his own proposal to restore Sr. Molina Ureña to the provisional Presidency. He therefore replied: "No, I cannot. If I return, I would be the President."

In an interview with Homer Bigart in the New York *Times* of May 6, 1965, Chancellor Benítez recalled: "Twice, Bosch said he'd be willing to go if that would avoid a frontal clash, but Martin said that he would only get himself killed."

According to Bosch and Benítez, who were the only other ones present, then, Martin's account was the kind of half-truth that results in a total falsehood. Also, Bosch emphasized, he had already, forty-eight hours earlier, asked Abe Fortas to arrange for a plane to transport him to Santo Domingo without having received a reply. In his mind, the United States clearly did not wish him to go back, and an anti-Bosch campaign in the United States was attributing to him all sorts of unworthy reasons for not wishing to go back. A difficult political decision was transformed into a simple failure of nerve.[*]

156

---

[*] The best explanation that I have seen for Bosch's decision at this time appeared in a letter to the San Juan *Star* of July 21, 1965, by Chancellor Benítez: "The issue is not one of courage as has been invidiously suggested elsewhere. In many ways Mr. Bosch is much more courageous than any one of us. His per-

After the second exchange about Bosch's possible return, the Dominican leader says that Mr. Martin received a telephone call from Washington. When he came back, according to Bosch, he attempted to get Bosch to issue a message to the Dominican people which would acknowledge that the revolution had fallen into Communist hands and accept this as justification for the landing of U.S. troops. Bosch says he was so astonished that he did not hear the other points Martin went on to dictate to him. Bosch heatedly told the U.S. emissary that he was "not an American functionary and Washington cannot dictate

sonal life fully supports this. It is rather a matter of intimate outlook, of emotional and intellectual reactions to dead-end situations which our tragic times force upon many of us. In Mr. Bosch's estimation he could only return during his unexpired term to the Dominican Republic as President or not at all. In 1963 he had chosen exile rather than precipitate a blood bath in Santo Domingo. He could not discard the possibility that his presence in the midst of conflict might intensify one now. Furthermore, Bosch resents bitterly American occupation, broods over his anticipation that it may last several years, and often says it is not within himself to deal personally and constructively with such an occupation. At the same time he cannot seal himself off from what is happening, for it is happening to his country, his people and himself." It should be noted that Dr. Benítez did not by any means see eye to eye with Bosch on everything. Of all the attacks on Bosch, however, the dregs were reached by William F. Buckley, Jr. In his column of June 1, 1965, he wrote that Bosch's "enormous personal weaknesses" suggested "even the possibility of dysphasia, or senility."

what I must do." Bosch states that Chancellor Benítez intervened and succeeded in convincing the former ambassador that Bosch was right.

Martin left all this out of his *Life* article. In his book, he relates that the Washington telephone call came from Abe Fortas who first suggested that "Bosch issue a statement now, saying he recognized the danger of a Castro/Communist takeover and the need to eliminate it, calling for an end to killing and the resumption of public services, and accepting the presence of U.S. forces for a minimum period needed to keep order" (p. 679). This is a watered-down version of the story first told by Bosch and, in essence, confirmed that Bosch was asked to subscribe to the "Communist danger" and U.S. intervention. Since Martin had already committed himself publicly to the "Communist takeover," not merely the danger, and Bosch had already denounced the U.S. intervention, precisely because he considered the entire Communist issue an indefensible red herring, it is hard to see how Martin or Fortas could have chosen to ask **158** him to sign a more obnoxious and self-destroying statement.

13

THE BEST MINDS OF THE JOHNSON ADMINISTRA-
tion went through three stages in their efforts
to make the idea of a Communist takeover of
the pro-Bosch revolt convincing.

At first, the numerical tendency was up-
ward—from 3 to 53 to 58, back to 54, and
finally to an altitude of 77. We have it from
the President that, when only eight Communists were reported to him, apparently on
April 28, "alerts were set up, and our men
continued to ferret out and study the organization" for more names, addresses, experience,
numbers, and backgrounds. Presumably the
authorities would not have gone to all this
trouble if they had not believed that numbers
were important. But only about a month later,
the holes punctured in the lists by the newsmen and the gradual realization that the numbers game was defeating its own end set the
numerical machinery in reverse.

In the second stage, the numbers began to move downward. Instead of trying to prove how dangerous a large number of Communists could be, the best minds labored to demonstrate how dangerous a very few Communists could be.

On May 26, Secretary of State Rusk hit back at critics of the administration's policy as follows:

> I am not impressed by the remark that there were several dozen known Communist leaders and that therefore this was not a very serious matter. There was a time when Hitler sat in a beer hall in Munich with seven people. And I just don't believe that one underestimates what can be done in chaos, in a situation of violence and chaos, by a few highly organized, highly trained people who know what they are about and know what they want to bring about.

Analogies soon became contagious. On the CBS television program of April 31, Ambassador Bennett brought up Castro:

> I don't think it's so important the actual number when one recalls that Fidel Castro first took to the hills with only twelve men. I think it's a question of training, of determined objectives and of being able to influence others who, for very legitimate motives, may be in the fight.

The Castro analogy was so appealing that Under Secretary Mann used it on Leonard Gross in *Look* of June 15: "Look at Cuba.

There were only twelve people in the beginning, and yet they took it over."*

When the administration's friends in the press began to work on this argument, the numbers proceeded to diminish almost to the vanishing point.

Raymond Moley in *Newsweek* of June 7, 1965, took the line that numbers did not count at all: "Another gripe is that there were only a 'few' Communists involved in the fighting. It was irrelevant whether there were 60 or 600 Communists involved."

In *The Reporter* of July 15, 1965, Selden Rodman got down to as low as two. In Santo Domingo, he related, he flung this crushing question at Héctor Aristy: "Did it take more than Raúl Castro and Che Guevara to guide the Cuban revolution into the Soviet fold?"

But if I were awarding a grand prize for this type of dialectics, it would undoubtedly go to the usually astute Eric Sevareid. In his

---

* As usual, these historical references were mangled even more brutally by the time they got to the Senate. Senator George Smathers improved on Mr. Mann as follows: "It has been admitted that there were only about 12 known Communist leaders in Cuba with Castro when he started his revolution" (*Congressional Record*, Senate, September 15, 1965, p. 23006). And to think that I have written two books that attempt to demonstrate (a) that Castro was a Castroite and not a Communist in 1956, (b) that the "twelve" were also Castroites and not "known Communists," and (c) that the official Communists disapproved of Castro's tactics before 1958!

column of May 30, he promulgated what may henceforth be known as "Sevareid's Law," which might be summed up as follows: the fewer Communists there are in a country, the more dangerous they are. Lest the reader think that I am being unfair to Mr. Sevareid, I hasten to quote his exact words:

> I fail to understand the editorialist who points out with disdain that after all, there were only a few handfuls of Communists present. In a very real sense their lack of numbers is their strength. It was because they were few that they could act with rapidity when the explosion came. It was because they were few that foreign opinion makers could make the Americans seem ridiculous and give us a propaganda defeat.

And so Mr. Sevareid had discovered a new and most dangerous form of the Communist conspiracy—to keep the number of Communists as low as possible. For, conversely, the more there are, the more likely they are to be dealt with severely, to be detected in their work, to act less rapidly, and to make it more difficult for foreign opinion-makers to make the Americans seem ridiculous. This line of reasoning clearly established Mr. Sevareid as the winner over Mr. Rodman by at least one point, downward.

One of the most disturbing aspects of the crisis, then, was not merely what the policy was, but how it was defended intellectually. When a Secretary of State thinks that he is justifying something as serious as U.S. military intervention in Latin America by reference to Hitler's "seven" and both the Under Secretary and the ambassador try to make the same point by evoking Castro's "twelve," it is necessary to ask: Is this the proper way to educate the American people to the real danger of Communism?

I suppose that Secretary Rusk was alluding to the fact that Adolf Hitler became member No. 7 of a committee of the German Workers' party in September 1919, usually considered the birth of the National Socialist movement.* It was an obscure little group at the time, that is true, but it was only one manifestation of a postwar German disease that was neither obscure nor little. Except for the somewhat ludicrous "beer hall *Putsch*" of 1923, Hitlerism did not become a serious menace until the world economic crisis of 1929, the increase of unemployment to six million, and the sensational upsurge of the Nazi party in the election of September 1930.

As for Castro, the legend of his "twelve" is equally dubious historically. There were 82

163

---

* As No. 7, Hitler must have sat in the Munich beer hall with only six people. Alan Bullock says that Hitler attended his first party meeting in a Munich beer-cellar with twenty or twenty-five people present (*Hitler: A Study in Tyranny,* p. 64).

with Castro aboard the yacht, *Granma,* when it completed its voyage to Cuba from Mexico in December 1956. After the disastrous landing, only a handful came together again in the Sierra Maestra. Castroite propaganda used to cite the number twelve, possibly to evoke the memory of twelve earlier disciples, but Castro himself subsequently reduced it to seven. In any event, almost half of the original contingent gradually reassembled in the Sierra Maestra and were joined by others. The anti-Bastista struggle had already been going on for over four years, and many different groups had taken part in it. To think of the seven or the twelve as having represented "the beginning" merely perpetuates the myth of Castro's monopoly of the struggle.

I do not think that this is sheer pedantry. Hitler's and Castro's rise to power should have been well enough known to leading officials of the State Department to have made them wary of such vulgarized and misleading popularizations.

But of course, the deeper issue was what the numbers meant, not how large they were. If **164** Mr. Rusk, Mr. Mann, and Mr. Bennett had sought to get across the idea that great and dangerous movements may begin with a few people and that they bear careful watching from the outset, there could be no objection. Yet many movements start with a handful and never change the course of history. Why do some succeed and others fail? The answer obviously does not lie in the prepotency of the few but in the social conditions which enable the few to become the many. If Hitler's "seven" or Castro's "twelve," to use the examples that have been given to us, remained seven and twelve, there would have been nothing more to worry about. But Hitler gained almost six-and-a-half million votes in 1930, and Castro capitalized on what became a truly national revulsion against the Batista regime.

Unfortunately, the purpose of these analogies with Hitler in 1919 and Castro in 1956 was not to warn against the *future* potentialities of such charismatic, demagogic figures. In the Dominican context, the analogies were rather intended to convey the idea that Hitler with seven men and Castro with twelve men were able to take over Germany and Cuba, even as a few Communists were allegedly able to take over the Dominican Republic. Something on the order of the U.S. landings in the Dominican Republic, it was suggested, should have taken place against Hitler's "seven" and Castro's "twelve." If we may trust Selden Rodman, moreover, not even Fidel was necessary; Raúl and Che had done it all by themselves.

At this late date, it really should not be necessary to restate the ABC of Castro's victory: Batista was overthrown because the Cuban people turned against him and his own henchmen deserted him, not because he was "defeated" by Castro's 12 men or 1200 men.

The *reductio ad absurdum* of these intellectual monstrosities was that the administration's defenders were forced to flaunt the specter of Communist supermen. If a few Communists could take over a revolt that had failed and in a few hours vanquish the entire Dominican military establishment, they were obviously a superior breed. In fact, in all Communist history, there had never been so few who had done so much so quickly against so many. At his press conference on May 26, 1965, Secretary Rusk emphasized that it was not the number of the Dominican Communists that had counted but their organization and training. On the CBS program of May 31, 1965, Under Secretary Mann reiterated that the actual number of Communists was not important—"it's a question of training, of determined objectives, and of being able to influence." Senator Lausche put it this way on September 17, 1965: "By skilled manipulation, propaganda, by assertion of leadership in

proper points, in street fighting, by aggressive activity, these Communists take hold. That is what they did in the Dominican Republic. A few skilled people can do this in the proper circumstances."

For a while, as I read these words, I wondered where I had seen them in somewhat different form before. Suddenly I realized that some of our foremost U.S. spokesmen had on this point become the faithful disciples of Ernesto Che Guevara. For more than any other Communist ideologist, Guevara had popularized the idea that a few revolutionists could take power, though even he had never gone so far as his *epigoni* in the State Department and U.S. Senate. Guevara had taught that a few revolutionists could *begin* the armed struggle for power, not that they could in a few hours or days successfully end it. The fact is that U.S. officials had and may still have a very vague notion of what happened in Santo Domingo on April 27 and 28 to cause the collapse of the Dominican armed forces, and they seized on this vulgarized form of "Guevara-ism" to give some credibility to the story that a few Communists had been responsible for both the collapse and the subsequent takeover of the revolt. The same U.S. sources, however, did not even make an effort to explain how victory-flushed Communist leaders could have decided to "withdraw from the scene" a week later without making a single effort to embroil the marines in a real battle.*

On at least two occasions, moreover, Under Secretary Mann suggested that the combined forces of the Soviet Union and Communist

---

* As put together later, an official U.S. day-by-day account of events in the Dominican Republic from

China were behind the Dominican Communists. In his interview with Max Frankel, Mr. Mann jointed out that "members of the Communist apparatus" were really an "instrument of Sino-Soviet military power." And on the CBS program, he again argued that U.S. passivity would have resulted in "a takeover of another island by the Sino-Soviet military bloc."

Could it be that no one had told the Under Secretary about the little discourtesies that had already made the "Sino-Soviet military bloc," if it ever existed, a thing of the past?

Finally, there came the third and last stage in the rationalization of U.S. policy. Instead of inflating the numbers of Dominican Communist supermen or insisting how strong a few could be, the new line sought to emphasize the weakness of the non-Communist opposition. This stage was neatly put in one sentence by Professor John N. Plank, a former State Department official, in *Foreign Affairs* (October 1965):

168

It should be noted, however, that President Johnson's intervention course was decided

---

April 24 to May 5 alleged that two of the Communist groups discussed the advisability of withdrawing their top leaders from open activity on May 4 and that the leaders of all three groups decided to withdraw on May 5 (*Congressional Record*, Senate, September 16, 1965, pp. 23311-14).

upon, not because of a judgment that the Communists in the Dominican Republic were strong, but rather because of a conclusion that non-Communist elements were too weak, too lacking in political sophistication, and too little skilled in the arts of governance, to withstand Communist infiltration and subsequent control.*

On the face of it, this was a far more sensible and moderate position. It seemed to avoid making the Dominican Communists too big or too small and introduced a seemingly more thoughtful element of relativity into the discussion. Nevertheless, it was, I think, only a variation on the original theme and it also brought out in bolder relief some of the most disagreeable aspects of U.S. policy.

I do not wish to go over already familiar ground—how weak the non-Communist elements really were, how much of their weakness was caused by U.S. policy, how much and for how long the Communists actually exercised "control." But had we earned the pretension of a superior "political sophistication"? It was assumed with disarming candor that President Johnson's intervention was justified because he and his advisers were endowed with a "political sophistication" in Dominican affairs denied to Juan Bosch and his

---

* Professor Plank himself was not in favor of the interventionist policy and merely tried to express the official position objectively.

supporters. I doubt whether anyone would care to dispute Mr. Johnson's "sophistication" in U.S. domestic politics, but I also doubt whether this sophistication has carried over to his conduct of foreign affairs in general and Latin American affairs in particular. Indeed, the U.S. handling of this Dominican crisis had been marked by such ineptitude and inconsistency that only the strongest power in the world could have afforded them. Political sophistication, like the strength of the Dominican Communists, is relative. But I question whether one student in a hundred of Latin American affairs believes that the United States had the political sophistication to carry off such tricky enterprises.

In the "arts of governance," for example, could we have given them what they lacked?

On the "Meet the Press" program of May 30, 1965, Secretary of State Rusk was asked about the re-establishment of the last Dominican constitution. The Secretary answered in part: "As you know, there is a very high controversy at the moment as between the constitution of 1963 and the constitution of 1962. In those circumstances, why not ask the Dominicans?"

From this, one might have gathered that there was a 1962 Dominican constitution comparable to the 1963 constitution and that both somehow enjoyed the same status. A Dominican could have given the Secretary a lesson in Dominican constitutional history.

It was in December 1960 that Trujillo promulgated his last constitution. It remained in force for the next two years, except for modifications by decree. These changes were mainly designed, after Trujillo's death in 1961, to remove articles dealing with the former dictator's special privileges and to enable the 1962 "Council of State" to rule and hold elections. The Council at first promised to convene a Constituent Assembly in August 1962 and to call general elections in December 1962. But it later changed its mind and decided to hold the elections first. As a result, the pro-Bosch landslide enabled an overwhelmingly pro-Bosch Congress to draw up the new constitution, something which the Council had not planned on.

Thus, in Dominican terms, the "constitution of 1962" was basically a relic of the Trujillo era. The "constitution of 1963" was the first democratically enacted document in almost forty years. This is what the "very high controversy" was essentially about.

But Max Frankel of the New York *Times* would not let the matter rest. He asked: "Why don't we now simply go back, since we are shooting for elections, to the only government that has been elected in that country within the past three years, actually?"

Mr. Rusk then gave the Dominicans more

free tutelage in the "arts of governance":
"That government lasted seven months, Mr.
Frankel. What is important about a constitution in the government is that it have the consent of the people at the time, of the day."

According to this principle, whenever a democratically elected government and a democratically enacted constitution are overthrown by force, the slate is wiped clean and the *golpistas* have the right to demand "consent" to a new constitution. Every coup, in effect, automatically voids the "consent" given to the previous constitution, however democratically enacted.

Nothing, to my mind, revealed the abyss that separated the U.S. official mind from the national aspirations of the Dominican people as much as this insensitivity to the meaning of the 1963 constitution.

For most of its history, the Dominican Republic had been a nation in name only. No sooner was it liberated from Haiti in 1844 than it became the plaything of one *caudillo* after another, one junta after another. Insurrection after insurrection, assassination after assassination, frustrated hope after frustrated hope—these were its lot. I know of no nation in Latin America, with the possible exception of its neighbor, Haiti, which has had such a disastrous past. From 1930, for thirty-one endless, remorseless, monstrous years, it was one man's chattel—a private fief, not a nation. In all this time, sophisticated American politicians paid homage to and demeaned themselves before the aging tyrant. His paid Washington adviser, Joseph E. Davies, was appointed U.S. ambassador to another tyrant in Moscow.

Trujillo's assassination in 1961 was, then, a unique moment in the decades-long agony of this people. For whatever reason, the door had opened on a new and better future. Were they to go through it to escape from the accursed cycle of coups, insurrections, juntas, despots, and *Jefes*? Or were they to fall back into the old pattern of self-appointed saviors who invariably became their exploiters and executioners?

This explains why the finest minds of Latin America have been filled with such a deep yearning for a constitutional solution to the still tormenting problem of political power and succession. Constitutional democracy is not merely the only way out of periodic bloodletting and dictatorship in all its forms; it is also the end of chatteldom, a reawakening of national consciousness, a rediscovery by a people of itself, and in the case of the Dominican Republic, the very beginning of a process of political self-realization that should have started over a hundred years ago.

For such a country and such a people, the free democratic elections of December 1962 and the democratically enacted constitution of

April 1963 were promises, above all, of a new national destiny. It did not matter so much that the constitution was not perfect (which is?) or that the President had his share of human defects (which one has not?). The constitution provided for its own amendment, and the President could be changed every four years. That is why the reaffirmation of the 1963 constitution was the banner and symbol of this revolt, why it was not a step backward but a step forward.

And then to tell the Dominican people that a tyrant's constitution enjoyed the same status as a democratically-enacted constitution, that the first democratic constitution they had had in almost forty years was simply voided by a coup, that there must be an infernal rhythm of coup and "consent," coup and "consent," that the provisions of a constitution are not binding if they are "highly controversial"—was this the way to teach the "arts of governance" to the poor natives too little skilled in them?

14

ONE THING THE UNITED STATES DID SUCCEED IN doing was disillusioning one Dominican leader after another.

The United States thought well enough of Donald Reid Cabral to invest a great deal of treasure and prestige in him. When he asked for U.S. intervention on the morning of April 25, he was permitted to fade away without a word of condolence. Nor did the new Provisional President, José Rafael Molina Ureña, get any U.S. sympathy on April 25 and 26; he was snubbed as a usurper or brushed off as a Communist front. Instead, our first hero was General Wessin y Wessin. *Time* magazine, which huckstered every twist and turn of the U.S. line most shamelessly, gave him its *de luxe* build-up (May 7, 1965). No secret was made of the fact that General Wessin was the strong man behind the three-man junta headed by Colonel Benoit, which the C.I.A. accredited on April 28.

But in Washington, a different solution of the Dominican crisis was soon in the making. On April 29, three Latin American advisers, former Costa Rican President José Figueres, former Venezuelan President Rómulo Betancourt, and former Puerto Rican Governor Luis Muñoz Marín, were brought to the White House. They were encouraged to act as an "informal committee" to consult with the Organization of American States (O.A.S.), the U.S. government, and Juan Bosch.

Sr. Figueres got in touch with Bosch in Puerto Rico and in conversations lasting two days they began to work out a new understanding. After two more weeks of these telephone negotiations, they arrived, in Figueres's words, at the following formula: "constitutional government, without Communism and without Trujilloism." The White House, Figueres says, "agreed with the objectives."*

After April 29, therefore, a struggle went on in Washington for the conscience and comprehension of President Johnson and those closest to him. If some of them had not been

* An English translation of Sr. Figueres's account may be found in the pamphlet, *Dominican Republic: A Study in the New Imperialism*, pp. 43-56. It is a particularly thoughtful and penetrating analysis of the Dominican problem. On May 2, 1965, President Johnson said: "We are in contact with such distinguished Latin American statesmen as Rómulo Betancourt and José Figueres. We are seeking their wisdom and their counsel and their advice."

deeply disturbed by the events and their own part in them, they would not have gone to the trouble of bringing three of the most respected and most progressive Latin American elder statesmen to advise them. In effect, one arm of U.S. policy was working against Bosch and one arm was tentatively working with him. On the night of May 2, as we have already seen, special Presidential emissary John Bartlow Martin told Juan Bosch that "his party had fallen under the domination of adventurers and Castro-Communists," and Martin went off the following day to concoct a new junta with Antonio Imbert at the head of it. It was inducted on May 7, and the benediction was given by *Time* (May 14)—"a Dominican national hero, Antonio Imbert Barreras."

But from various quarters—the news correspondents in the Dominican Republic, the three Latin American consultants, and probably its own intelligence sources—Washington began to hear that perhaps Tony Imbert was not quite the right man for the job. He was not such a national hero, after all, despite his part in the assassination of Trujillo. Politically he was trusted by no one. Socially his base was just as narrow as Wessin's or Benoit's. Thus the Figueres-Bosch telephone negotiations were not discouraged, and within days after Imbert had been set up in business, the last thing that one would have expected to happen, considering the foregoing, happened—a decision was made in Washington to dump Imbert and to go back to an understanding with Bosch.

The President's *homme de confiance*, Abe Fortas, according to Tad Szulc, arrived incognito in San Juan, Puerto Rico, on May 13. He met with Chancellor Jaime Benítez, after which they went to see Juan Bosch. The basic formula had already been worked out in the Figueres-Bosch telephone negotiations: a "constitutional government, without Communism and without Trujilloism." Bosch himself was eliminated from consideration as the head of such a government, but the problem arose whether it should not, in some sense, derive from Bosch's 1963 government. According to Szulc, Bosch proposed as head of the new government his former Minister of Agriculture and a successful Dominican businessman, Silvestre Antonio Guzmán. Mr. Fortas, soon to be appointed a Supreme Court Justice by President Johnson, allegedly made no commitments and flew back to Washington to report to the President.

Within about twenty-four hours, the President acted on Mr. Fortas's report. He appointed a team of four—a team that could hardly have been more impressive—to go to San Juan and Santo Domingo. They were Special Assistant on National Security Affairs McGeorge Bundy, Under Secretary of State

Thomas Mann, Assistant Secretary of State Jack Hood Vaughn, and Deputy Secretary of Defense Cyrus R. Vance. Mann and Vaughn apparently did no more than stop in Puerto Rico en route to the Dominican Republic. Vance remained at the air force base in Puerto Rico. The negotiations with Sr. Bosch were conducted entirely by Mr. Bundy. I have been assured by a person who was present at all the discussions between them that Sr. Guzmán had been agreed upon in advance. Colonel Fernández Domínguez, who was Bosch's chief military adviser in Puerto Rico and who was slated to become the Minister of Interior and Police in the proposed Guzmán cabinet, had previously been sent to Santo Domingo to confer with Colonel Caamaño and, with his agreement, to arrange for Sr. Guzmán's presence in Puerto Rico. Sr. Guzmán was flown to San Juan in a U.S. military plane earlier in the day, and he as well as Bosch and Benítez were present at the discussions with Bundy. (Colonel Fernández returned to Santo Domingo on May 19 and was shot to death by U.S. soldiers in a tragic, still controversial incident.)

179

Sr. Guzman, I have been informed, was a "compromise" as far as Washington and Bosch were concerned. Bosch and Bundy, it appears, quickly learned to respect each other's qualities and good faith. Guzmán was also flown to Washington for consultations. Bundy and

Vance, expressing confidence in the Guzmán plan's success, left for Santo Domingo on May 16. If ever the United States seemed committed to a course of action, this was it.

The Guzmán plan was presented to the top Dominican air force, navy, and army commanders on May 18. As might have been expected, they were not happy with it and saw no reason to replace Imbert's set-up. Under Secretary Mann flew back to Washington that day. Bundy, Vaughn, and Vance carried on in Santo Domingo. By May 19, the Dominican military were virtually accusing the Bundy mission of a sellout to the Communists. Hal Hendrix quoted them as saying that the United States wanted "to turn this country over to Communism" and was putting pressure on them to accept "persons of Communist affiliation or sympathizers."* At the same time, Imbert saw fit to push a military offensive against Caamaño's forces in the northern sector of the capital. In telephone calls to Washington, Szulc states, Bundy referred to Imbert first as "Napoleon" and then as "Frankenstein." The cost of this embroglio to

---

*It should be noted that Chancellor Jaime Benítez went along with the Bundy mission to Santo Domingo. On this point, he later wrote: "This tragedy is much different from the previous one in Cuba with which—because of thoughtlessness, or obsession, or faulty information—it was at first confused" (*Saturday Review*, July 17, 1965). It is hard to think of anyone who is less of an innocent in these matters.

the United States was about $21,000,000 for May and June alone.

It seemed incredible that Imbert's junta, which depended on U.S. largesse, should defy the United States until it was revealed that the United States paid the junta to do what it was tempted to do itself. On the basis of official testimony before the Senate Foreign Relations Committee, Max Frankel later revealed that the Johnson administration "considered an attack to wipe out the rebel force and was deterred only because of the high number of casualties it would have inflicted on women and children."*

Thus, the struggle over the Bundy mission in Santo Domingo was both a factor in, and a reflection of, a similar struggle that was going on in Washington. On Sunday, May 23, Mr. Bundy received a message from Washington which torpedoed his entire mission.† This

---

* New York *Times*, November 14, 1965. All the witnesses before the committee, with one exception, were administration officials: Secretary of State Rusk, Under Secretary of State Mann, Deputy Secretary of Defense Vance, Ambassador Bennett, C.I.A. Director Admiral Raborn, and Assistant Secretary of State Vaughn. The only non-Government but not unfriendly witness was former Governor of Puerto Rico Luis Muñoz Marín.

† This message apparently contained three demands which Washington knew in advance were unacceptable. Sr. Guzmán had agreed to base his government on anti-Communism and anti-Trujilloism, and to make both clear in his first address. But one of the

message was the result of influences brought to bear on President Johnson, who was finally swayed by another of Secretary of State Rusk's incongruous historical analogies. Mr. Rusk apparently succeeded in talking Mr. Johnson out of the Guzmán plan by dredging up the unfortunate consequences of Sumner Welles's efforts to make and unmake governments in Cuba back in 1933. A lengthy memorandum, according to Tad Szulc, was drawn up in the State Department on these Cuban events of over thirty years ago; it must be the

---

points demanded that he should also agree to the expulsion from the country of a number of Communists in express violation of the 1963 constitution which forbade the Trujillo practice of exiling opponents for political reasons. Article 66 of the 1963 constitution stated: "No Dominican can be expelled from the country. The deportation or expulsion of any foreigner from Dominican territory can only take place as a result of a sentence handed down by a competent tribunal with the observance of legal formalities and procedures." Another point sought to tie Sr. Guzmán's hands with respect to the future armed force's command. The Dominicans were dumbfounded of course, to be confronted by U.S. "conditions," which, if meant in good faith, should have been presented to them at a much earlier stage of the negotiations. In addition, the proposed Guzmán government was expected to do the United States' bidding even before it was formed, while the United States was still protesting publicly that it did not, could not, and would not interfere in Dominican affairs. The circumstances leading up to the May 23 message made clear that it was intended to torpedo the Bundy mission, and it was so interpreted by Dr. Benítez, who was with Mr. Bundy during this period.

first repudiation of Sumner Welles's activities in an official document. After the C.I.A.'s role in giving birth to the Benoit junta and John Bartlow Martin's vaunted mid-wifery of the Imbert junta, the persuasiveness of this argument against Antonio Guzmán is surely of psychological as well as of historical interest. In any event, the only one on the U.S. side who seems to have come out of this particular incident with some honor is McGeorge Bundy.

At the time, the exact sequence of these events was confused by what was probably the most outrageous journalistic scandal of all. On May 24, 1965, the Washington *Daily News* and New York *World-Telegram and Sun* appeared with an article by the former's editor, John O'Rourke, accusing Antonio Guzmán of financial malfeasance as director of a government bank and, therefore, obviously unfit to be the head of a new Dominican government. When reporters asked the State Department for comment on the story, the spokesman cryptically replied that "it is up to Mr. Guzmán to explain his role in the bank." The least that can be said of this answer is that it did not suggest any undue confidence on the part of the State Department in the probity of the man whom it had approached to become the next Dominican President. Since Guzmán's candidacy was obviously cooling off in Washington at this very time, the charge of financial "irregularities" seemed to be linked with it. Within forty-eight hours, the bank's auditors and everyone concerned with the alleged misconduct had denied that there was any truth in it. The story had been planted by a paid agent during Reid Cabral's regime of the Dominican Embassy in Washington. It had been knocking around the State Department for some time, as had the audit of the bank's books. At his press conference on May 26, Secretary of State Rusk came forth with one of his masterly understatements: "We have no information ourselves indicating irregularities on Mr. Guzmán's part." It is hard to believe that the editor of a Washington newspaper would not have consulted someone in the State Department's top echelon before signing his name to a story which, if without foundation, was bound to blow up in his face. At any rate, the O'Rourke story was a consequence, not a cause, of the decision to abandon Guzmán.

At the same news conference, Mr. Rusk also led the press to believe that the State Department had been talking with Sr. Guzmán "about the possibilities of a coalition government." Such a coalition, the Secretary explained, had to be based "upon a broad agreement among different political elements." Thereafter, the newspapers attributed the failure of the Guzmán plan to the fact that the Imbert group had refused to accept it.